By
Dennis F.

<u>Acknowledgments</u>

I would first and foremost like to thank my family for the patience they had while I prepared, these recipes. My dear wife Robin, for all my tantrums, all the samples (even when she was not so fond of them), being woken up in the middle of the night with my new ideas that then, meant nothing to her. Especially after all the clean ups I left behind for her to tend to. My daughters, some of the samples were a real challenge for them. The patience and courage they had while tasting my new recipes, I know sometimes they were very courageous allowing me to have them to try a few. To my "Pops", the late Emanuel John Spiteri, all the time he spent with me, drilling me with the fundamentals, even when I thought he was wrong, he kept quite until I proved myself wrong. To My mother Olga, for looking the other way as I destroyed the kitchen when I was a young man experimenting in her kitchen. My grandmother placing a chair next to her so that I may examine every step in the meals she prepared. My grandfather for giving me credit whenever or whatever I served him, He always made me feel as if I had accomplished something. The Detroit Athletic Club, where I received my first professional job as a cook, the chef and cooks in the early to mid seventies for taking interests in me and showing me the ropes, especially one, my dearest and closest friends the late Charlie "The Goose" Cauchi, we spent many times together, as brothers, friends and work mates. He always made sure to look over me whatever we did; he was the big brother I never had. I also would like to thank some of my very special friends for allowing me to go into their family archives and retrieve there recipes, for one, Michael Gemus (Lionel's son), for providing me his family's cookbook which his parents took an immense amount of time and effort to publish. I thank a great friend, Tom "Dillybilly" Dill for spending countless hours perfecting the arts and techniques of smoking meats, and for creating his own barbeque sauces and rubs, which he allowed me to introduce them in my cookbook. Last but definitely not least, my closest and dearest mentor Rita Vella Cruz, for spending long nights in front of her computer proof reading and correcting all my mistakes. No matter what predicament I got into, or how frustrated I became, Rita always gave me positive advice, and never permitted me to give up.

1

Contents

GROWING UP IN CORKTOWN

I grew up in small neighborhood in Detroit known as Corktown. Corktown is an area just West of Downtown Detroit where many Maltese people migrated throughout WWII to come to work for the thriving automobile industry. My grandfather shortly after marring my grandmother needed work to support his growing family, left Malta and migrating to Detroit. Once having stable employment, at the Chrysler Motor Car Factory, he called for my grandmother and there children to the new world.

My father, left his family in Malta at age 17 where he came to New York in the late 1940's to help his uncle start a small Maltese restaurant in Astoria, near Queens. Finally residing in Detroit, he met and wed my mother. He owned several, small "hamburger joints" and was one of the first to bring the industrial catering (lunch wagons) to the Metropolitan Detroit area in the early 1960's.

My mother arrived in the United States at age 5. In the days of the depression, school was not the most important agenda. But she managed to finish high school and worked at Hutzel hospital as a candy striper, she then married my father, and her career in the employment world soon was over. She began to help out in the small restaurants they owned.

The Maltese community migrated to Corktown and began to started their own church and clubs, making Corktown their home away from home. Today Corktown is very unique; it is located in the middle of an inner city occupied with a multi ethnic background. Corktown has always held its own weight against the crime and trauma of inner city lifestyles. It was an experience growing up in Corktown, where most of my pals were Maltese, And Hispanic. The Maltese kids spoke the language and going from one house to another to eat four or five Maltese meals in a given day. There rarely were any other types of ethnic meals on the tables except for the traditional Maltese recipes. Once in a while someone would venture out and prepare a typical American dish, such as meatloaf, fried chicken, or a typical outdoor barbeque of ribs, hamburgers, and hot dogs. We did visit our Hispanic friends for a great meal.

This is where I begin my venture; I always had a passion to cook. From sitting at the kitchen table at age 6, watching my Nana (grandmother) make the traditional pastizzi. To preparing my Nanu (grandfather), a typical Maltese breakfast of a few boiled eggs and a half of a loaf of crusty bread with tomatoes.

In my early teens, I helped my father cater different function for his clients he serviced in the industrial catering business during the holiday. I can also remember my Pops taking over above the Maltese club's kitchen. He then began to prepare meals for the single men that also came to the United States for employment later in the 60's and 70's. The main flow of Maltese people coming to America lasted from the early 1940's until the late 1960's, when Detroit was really the motor city and employment in the automobile industry flourished.

After graduating high school from Holy Redeemer High in Detroit, my father suggested I quit the Detroit Athletic Club, where I started as a cook's help. To except a job as an apprentice for a local

3

tool and die shop. I lasted three months. I kept insisting to my parents, that I wanted to cook professionally and someday own my own restaurant. My father always seemed to discourage me, wanting me to have a more stable, higher paying career, his excuse was cooks were "dime a dozen". I then began to I managed a Coney Island restaurant just down from what used to be Tiger Stadium. That gave me the experience of managing a busy, fast passed restaurant.

My father accepted me as a partner in his mobile industrial catering business at the young age of 19, shortly after, marrying my wife Robin. We shared all the tasks amongst the three of us. After 11 years in the business, I decided to go back to the restaurant business, this time as an owner. I opened my first Deli in Bloomfield Hills, Michigan. It was a typical deli of the mid 1980's. .

I sold the deli after getting tired of the commute. I wanted to emphasize more to residential and commercial catering. I did that for 21 years while fiddling with a few small restaurants around Downtown Detroit, again packing them to capacity. I owned a small quaint, carry-out deli that served meals in the back of a market. I worked with lady (Lorraine) from Mississippi that taught me how to make delicious soul food. Lorraine showed me how to put "grandma's toe in it"

I always wanted to write a cookbook of my ethnic background. I realized that there is such a large Maltese-American population that would enjoy savoring Maltese cuisine, as our parents or grandparents prepared.

I began to think of a way other people could enjoy Maltese recipe's without being hesitant. I started to brainstorm and modify certain recipes. Once It worked out, I revised the traditional recipes, after preparing experimental meals for my family; I started to invite friends over for dinner. I have great respect for traditional Maltese cuisine, but if you have not been raised on it, as in every traditional Ethnic recipe, sometimes the recipes can be overwhelming.

I decided I would write a cook book of recipes from around the world, but predominantly Maltese recipes that I grew up on. I didn't want this cookbook to be so formal, I wanted the average cook to come home after a day at work and open this book to a recipe, and not be afraid to try it. It is also a menagerie of recipes that I have gathered from close family and friends (some recipes are named after). They are recipes that while visiting, their homes or functions, are recipes that stay with me.

My mission is to help someone. It is not intended for one to seldom use this book; it is not intended be used just for special occasions. I want to make it simple enough to prepare a wholesome meal after a tired day at work, or one can prepare a more extravagant meal when there is more time to do this. I hope you and your family can enjoy most of these recipes, I don't expect to satisfy all, but if I can satisfy your taste most of the time, my job is accomplished.

Bon Appetito,
Dennis Felix Spiteri

Presentation, flavor and the correct amount.

I have been preparing as I mention throughout this book, daily meals for my family of five to a function with hundreds of guests. I understand that it is easy to follow a recipe, no matter how difficult it is, or how much time it may take. As long as you follow the directions, you shouldn't run into any predicaments.

I realize the main concern for a novice cook preparing for a function or a meal, is the infamous question, will this be enough? In this short but informative section, are the guidelines which I stand behind. In most cases, it will help you prepare the proper amount. Take into consideration, of the surroundings the function will take place in, and what type of guests they are, families, just adults, or all children? Which should tell you if they are big eaters or not. It may be a sunny outdoor picnic or an indoor get together. I always state throughout this book, "Do what makes you feel comfortable", if you feel this recipe is not enough, go ahead and make a little more, I always believed that it is best to have leftovers, then to have guests leave hungry. Remember, it is most important to make yourself, feel good about your event. You as the host are the most important person.

It is very important to understand what will hold up in different temperatures, what is safe. You can make your guests quite ill if these rules are not followed. Take this into consideration, and stay away from mayonnaise based recipes when the temperature will be warm. Potato salad for instance, in the hot sun can become deadly to you guests. Instead, consider serving baked beans, or German potato salad. This is a good rule to follow. If you are going to serve your guests for more than a few hours, try to serve what holds longer without little or any refrigeration. If you are adamant on serving food that should be kept cool, I suggest using some type of iced filled trays or bowls under the serving dishes, or keep them in a cooler. For warmer foods, chaffing dishes work best.

As a general rule, choose food that will offer a variety of texture, color, and flavor. Presentation is the first impression your guest will embed in their mind before they taste your dish. Your guests will make a judgment to either to try it or not. I have seen time and time again, a delicious dish prepared perfectly, but the presentation was not properly orchestrated. This is the result in the guest shying away. It is funny, I have also seen simple appetizers like a popcorn shrimp carefully placed on Melba toast with slice of cucumber over a mayonnaise based dressing, made the guests rave about it.

Make a shopping list well in advance and be prepared to spend some time doing this thoroughly. Always check the availability of unusual ingredients (I try to stay away from recipes that call for such). Hunting around at the last minute can be quite irritatingly and time consuming. Suppliers tend to be eager to let you know what foods are available all year round, but when it comes time to shop, there can be some obscure reason why they don't have what you inquire. It is far better to change you menu in enough time to allow you if needed to improvise. When it comes to preparation, the speediest method of preparing from a cocktail party to a major function is undoubtedly by the proper production line method. Always keep in mind what needs to be chilled or frozen first, is where you start, so that other recipes can be prepared while the recipe(s) are chilling or freezing.

The choices on the menu should tell you how many and whether waiters or waitresses will be needed to serve the party. If there is to be no help at all, it is best to limit the choice of food to five items per course. If you are providing a wait staff, allow one waiter per twenty five guests for food, and one bartender for every thirty guests. For limited beverages, one bartender per fifty guests will do.

The number of guests will determine the amount of food you purchase. Here is what I have found to be the most precise amounts. <u>THERE ARE NONE</u>! If you are catering for a profit, and for a large gathering, then yes it is crucial what to purchase so that you do not go ever your budget. If you ask your meat provider of the specific meat being served, he/she will give you a good idea of how many ounces per person. Again, take into consideration of the crowd, for example a bridal shower with the same menu as a super bowl party will use a considerable less amount of food. Rule of thumb is 4 – 6 ounces of each meat per person if two meats are being served, 3 - 4 ounces each if more than two meats are being served. 1 - 2 cups each, of potato, or, 1 baked per person (allow 5% for mistakes). It is safe to calculate 2/3 cups for each vegetable per person. 1 ½ rolls per person, 2 slices of bread per person unless cold cuts are on the menu, then 4 slices per person.

Don't hesitate to read the label on the container, it is usually is a good guideline. If the function is a friendlier gathering, instead for a profit, then you should be able to know how much your guests can eat. I may want to impress my friends with a 16 oz. steak on the grill instead following the rule of thumb and serve them a 6 to 8 oz. steak. For my personal guests, I would much rather see impressive smiles than frowns. Remember everyone loves to take a little leftover home. Remember always allow 5% for mistakes. We all make mistakes.

Deciding on how much drink to supply can be a tricky question. It would be disastrous for a cocktail party to run dry. Most neighborhood liquor stores will allow you to buy in excess with the understanding of returning the unopened bottles for a complete refund. My solution you ask? B.Y.O.B. It also very important to have a good idea of what type of liquor your guests drink. For example, I have had a bottle of gin sitting on my shelf for ages, but I always keep a few fifths of a Canadian whiskey, Amaretto, and Captain Morgan's spiced rum.

The following page is an example of the bar supplies for a party that I had for 100 guests during Christmas, where the drinks are flowing freely all evening:

2 Bottles each:
Red, White and White Zinfandel Wines
Vodka
Rum

1 Bottle each:
Scotch
Bourbon
Whiskey
Bourbon
Gin
Peach Snapps
Apple Snapps
Sweet Vermouth
Tequila
Amaretto

Supplies/Mixers:

Ginger Ale	Lemon Lime soda	Cola	Diet Cola
Tonic Water	Sweet & Sour Mix	Soda Water	Orange Juice
Cranberry	Milk	Sugar	Salt
Grapefruit	Grenadine	Coconut Milk	Pineapple Juice

Lemons, limes, orange, slices, maraschino cherries, stir straws, and olives.

If your bar has been stocked with the above supplies, you will be able to make most popular drinks. I suggest having a basic bartenders guide handy.

If there is not sufficient refrigerator space available to chill your bar supplies, I suggest a cooler as close as possible filled with ice cubes and another cooler to serve the ice out of. Also have on hand, plenty of cold water, a blender, measuring shot glass, shaker, and strainer. A wine cooler is always impressive to your guests. Coffee with condiments never hurts toward the end of the event.

For the flatware and glassware, allow 1 ¼ dinner plate, 2 ½ salad/appetizer plates (if appetizers are served), 2 regular drinking glasses, 2 mixed glasses, 5% of wine glasses, and 15% of shot glasses per guests.

Barbeque Sauces, Mops, and Rubs

I have tested every recipe in this section. There is a great deal of pride within this cookbook, but this segment is where it all comes out.

Dark Beer Mop

I like using this particular mop when smoking chicken and pork. The beer gives it a distinctive flavor.

1 large chopped red onion
4 -6 cloves chopped garlic
3 Serrano chilies
4 bottles dark beer
¼ cup brown sugar
2 bay leaves
1 tablespoons kosher salt
2 tablespoons freshly ground black pepper

Place all ingredients in a saucepan and simmer over medium heat
For 15 minutes.
Allow to cool before using.

Dennis' Bar- B- Queue Mop

This may sound too simple, but it works well with all types of meats and poultry. I have tried to add this or that, but in the long run, this is a simpler recipe that worked best.

1½ cup apple cider vinegar
1cup balsamic vinegar (Rendered down to a ½ cup works best)
2 tablespoons white pepper
4 tablespoons Tabasco sauce
1 12 oz. can Dr. pepper soda
1 cup prune juice (optional)
1 stick butter
½ cup molasses
½ cup pure cane syrup
¼ cup soy sauce

Simmer very slowly, the balsamic vinegar until it reaches ½ the amount.
Heat on a very low heat and whip together until butter is melted
And all is mixed well.

Curried Barbeque Sauce

This is my sauce that mostly resembles my dark-sweet Bar B Queue sauce. I knew that I someday would need a sauce that would accompany lamb, so what I thought of was to combine a sweet taste with a curried background. This sauce works best when used with lamb, mutton or even Bar B Queued goat, but can be used on poultry. Careful using the chili paste, this is extremely hot.

1 large (40) oz. tomato catsup
2 tablespoons of each of the following:
   cayenne pepper
   Allspice
4 tablespoons curry powder
3 tablespoons of each of the following:
   garlic powder
   onion powder
   kosher salt
   black pepper
   white pepper
3-4 tablespoons Tabasco sauce
1½ cup apple cider vinegar
¾ cups brown sugar
½ cup margarine
¼ cup of each as follows:
   chili powder
Thai chili paste to taste (optional)

Mix wet ingredients together wet, simmer, add dry ingredients and simmer an additional 45 minutes. Store for at least 2 days before using.

Dennis' Dark Robust Barbeque Sauce

The reason this barbeque sauce has this name is because of the cola mixing with the tangy, spicy salty ingredients. I enjoy this sauce mostly on beef, don't be afraid using it on all other red meats and poultry. My wife likes this sauce the best on her chicken. My youngest daughter Ashley loves it on baked potatoes and even on her fries. Prepare it and judge the taste for yourself. I found that when I stored it for a few days, the taste seemed to be more flavorful, and aromatic.

1 large (40) oz. tomato catsup
1 12 oz. Can Cola
2 tablespoons of each of the following:
  cayenne pepper
  allspice
3 tablespoons of each of the following:
  garlic powder
  onion powder
  kosher salt
  black pepper
  white pepper
  Italian spices
3-4 tablespoons Tabasco sauce
1½ cup apple cider vinegar
¾ cups brown sugar
½ cup margarine
½ cup Molasses
¼ cup of each as follows:
  white grape or apple juice
  pineapple juice
  chili Powder
1/8 cup vanilla
Thai chili paste to taste (optional)

Mix wet ingredients together wet, simmer, add dry ingredients and simmer an additional 45 minutes. Store for at least 2 days before using.

Polynesian Barbeque Sauce

This is a Bar B Queue sauce that has its own distinctive flavor. I tried it on shrimp. It brought out the flavor very well not hiding the delicate flavor of the shrimp. I even deep fried the shrimp and used it as a dipping sauce instead of the traditional cocktail sauce. Everyone who tasted also preferred it over traditional cocktail sauce. I tried it on other fish such as, whitefish, scallops, sea bass, and many other different light flesh fish. I enjoy using this sauce when grilling more delicate seafood, it tends to bring out the flavor. My oldest daughter Stacy likes grilling chicken with it and drizzle it over white rice.

4 cups pureed pineapple
2 cups coconut milk (COCO Lopez)
2 cups Teriyaki marinade
1½ cups apple cider vinegar
1 cup orange juice (with pulp is better)
1 cup brown sugar
½ cup white sugar
½ cup honey
½ soy sauce
¼ cup kosher salt
¼ cup flour or arrowroot (to thicken)
4 tablespoons Tabasco
4 tablespoons white pepper

Mix together except for the thickening agent. Simmer for 45 minutes and thicken with the flour or arrowroot. Cool and store for at least 3 days before using, so that the ingredients will marry each other. You may use it once it chills, but I have stored this recipe for over a year in a tightly sealed jar in the refrigerator.

Dillbilly's Dry Rub

My good friend Tom Dill and I tried different rubs, and after experimenting with others, we think this is the most universal and best one. This rub works very well on all red meats and poultry.

1 cup brown sugar
2 oz. paprika
4 tablespoons granulated garlic
4 tablespoons onion powder
¼ cup Italian seasonings
1 cup western Bar-B-Queue seasonings (red meats only)
¼ cup poultry seasoning (poultry only)
¼ cup Jamaican jerk seasonings
¼ cup kosher salt
2 tablespoons black pepper
2 tablespoons white pepper
2 tablespoons chili powder

Add all ingredients in a metal mixing bowl and whip dry, until well blended.

Dillbilly's Wet Mop

This is a very basic wet mop Tom has perfected, works best with pork.

1 cup apple cider vinegar
1 cup balsamic vinegar
¼ cup Worchester sauce
2 tablespoons white pepper
4 tablespoons Tabasco
1 12oz. can cola
1 stick butter
¾ cup molasses
¼ cup pure cane sugar

Heat and mix over low flame until all ingredients are mix together, Chill overnight.

Oriental Marinade

This mop has what I call a universal flavor. It works with all types of meat and seafood.   Try it on cold noodles and top with green onion stems for an Oriental flair.

1 cup soy sauce
¼ cup sesame oil
¼ cup sugar
3 cloves garlic minced
1 tablespoon ground ginger
1 teaspoon cracked pepper

Combine all ingredients and blend well. This marinate is versatile, try it on salmon, pork, and chicken breasts.

Quick Marinade

Fast, and full of flavor. Works best with red meats.

12 oz. orange juice
12 oz. bottled lemon juice
2 cups vinegar
1½ Cups oil
½ cup water
2 tablespoons Worcestershire sauce
2 tablespoons salt
2 teaspoons Cracked pepper
2 teaspoons oregano
1 teaspoon 3 Cloves minced garlic

Combine all ingredients and use to marinate meats 2 hours to overnight (refrigerated) before cooking.

<u>Beverages:</u>

Starting off with a refreshing cocktail or an alcoholic punch adds a nice touch to any occasion. Keep in mind, Punch and virgin drinks can be made for the children.

Dennis' Apricot Wine

This is a good recipe for a novice bartender. This wine makes a great cocktail before a festive meal.

Note; this recipe requires the liquid to stand for at least thirty days before bottling.

1 lb. Dried apricots
4 quarts warm water
6½ cups white sugar
1½ cups seeded raisins
1 tablespoon ground ginger
2 medium lemons sliced thin
2 medium oranges sliced thin
½ yeast cake

Wash the apricots thoroughly and rinse at least 3 times, pat dry in a paper towel and cut them in half's.
Place them in a large crock and add the warm water, reserving a ½ cup for dissolving the yeast cake.
Stir in the sugar, fruits and ginger.
Add the now diluted yeast cake.
Cover the crock and let stand for at least thirty days, stirring the mixture only once every other day.
After thirty days or so this may be bottles.

Italian Fruit Punch

Everyone has their favorite recipe for fruit punch. Here is mine. Lemoncello is Italian lemon liquor, you can purchase from most liquor stores.

2 cups orange juice
2 cups chilled sparkling water
1/2 cup maraschino liqueur
1/4 cup limoncello
Ice
Black licorice, for garnish

Mango Lassi

Refreshing summers drink that everyone can enjoy. Sweet but yet tart, just a great combination of flavors that even that children can join in.

2 ripe, sweet mangos
11/2 cup plain nonfat yogurt
2 tablespoons honey
2 cups ice (1 tray of ice)

Peel and dice the mango and puree in the blender. Add the rest of the ingredients and puree until the ice is crushed and the drink is frothy. Serve in tall glasses with additional ice, if desired.

Old fashioned Holiday Egg Nog

This is a very old recipe going back to the early 1920's. My friend Tony's family made this for the holidays. Even the children were able to sample a glass.

1 heaping tablespoon white sugar
½ glass shaved ice
1 fresh egg
1 wine glass whiskey or rum
½ tumbler half and half
Shake thoroughly and strain.
Grate a small amount of nutmeg on top and serve.

Robin's Babylon Spice Drink

Make sure you have enough soaked ginger in the rum. This recipe makes only one drink. Multiply accordingly.

2 ounces fresh ginger, peeled and sliced
11/2 ounces rum
Ice cubes
1/2-ounce coconut milk
4 ounces mango juice
1-ounce grated coconut
1 maraschino cherry, for garnish
1 slice orange, for garnish

Soak the ginger in the rum for 24 hours. Place ice in a cocktail shaker. Add the ginger-rum mixture, coconut milk, and mango juice to the shaker. Shake well and strain into a large cocktail glass. Serve with a topping of the grated coconut, a cherry, and an orange slice on the lip of the glass. Serve immediately.

Sangria - Father Timothy D. Hogan

This recipe comes directly from the University of Salamanca. This wine beverage is full of flavor and aroma. Try it when serving a Spanish dish.

4 liters red wine
1 liter orange soda
¼ liter gin
¼ liter brandy
½ liter lemon juice
Thin sliced oranges
Thin sliced limes
Thin sliced peaches
Sprinkle cinnamon
1 lb. Sugar

Mix and set and cool for 3 to 4 hours

Sorrel Drink

An African/Caribbean drink made from ingredients that are plentiful in there region. A nice way to start off a Polynesian barbeque. Consider preparing different poultries and fish.

5 to 6 (1-inch) slices ginger
1 cup dried sorrel leaves
1 tablespoon cloves
Brown sugar
Red wine sherry, optional

Let cut ginger sit for 2 to 3 hours. The longer it sits the stronger it becomes. Boil ginger in 2 quarts of water. Once water is boiling, add sorrel and cloves. Boil for 30 minutes. Strain and add sugar and wine, to taste. Chill and serve.

*Sorrel is a plant that grows on trees. It is harvested around November and December and can be purchased pre-packaged from Caribbean or African stores.

Salad Dressings & Sauces

In this section you will find a menagerie of salad dressings and aromatic sauces. Preparing your own dressing and sauces will bring out the expertise at your table.

Basic Maltese Tomato Sauce

This is a quick savory tomato sauce. I use it for all pasta dishes that I do not want meat in. Sometimes, over angel hair pasta makes a nice light meal. This sauce is predominately used for ravioli. My family uses it to dip hard crust bread in.

1 Can Tomato sauce
1 Can Tomato puree`
1 Can Tomato paste
3 Cloves slivered garlic
1 Small onion
Extra virgin olive oil Salt & Pepper to taste

Sautee` in olive oil the onions and garlic (I have seen cooks remove the onions and garlic once the oil ha been flavored, I do not)
Stir in the paste and mix well
Add the other ingredients salt & pepper to taste, and simmer 30 minutes

Note:
This sauce can be frozen or canned

Dennis Olive Oil Pasta Sauce

This sauce must be prepared while tossed in with cooked pasta (Angel hair is my favorite). Quick and easy.

2 cups extra virgin olive oil
4 minced garlic
½ minced onion
3 teaspoons fresh parsley
3 tablespoons Italian seasonings

In a sauce pan sauté the onion and garlic quickly and toss in the cooked pasta.
Add the remaining ingredients, stirring often.
Top with parmesan cheese and serve with a hard crust loaf of bread and a tossed green salad.

Bordelaise Sauce

This is a delicious sauce to serve with steaks or other plain beef preparations. The sauce can be made days in advance or can be frozen in ice cube trays. The name "Bordelaise" probably is associated with Bordeaux wine which was more than likely used when the sauce originated. Any dry red wine will serve the purpose.

1 Medium onion chopped (or approx 5 scallions chopped up, greens included)
3 tablespoons Butter
1 cup Dry red wine
*12 oz. Beef base or Demi-glace
1 bay leaf
Thyme
Extra butter

In a large heavy skillet, melt the butter and sauté the onions on medium heat until they are soft but not brown.
Add the wine and allow to heat vigorously until the liquid is almost gone and the liquid is at a glaze stage; it should be bubbly and syrupy.
Add the beef base, the bay leaf and thyme, bring just to a boil, lower the heat and allow simmering for approximately 4 or 5 minutes. If desirable, add 2 tbsp of butter and stir until it has melted. Strain and store until further use.

Dennis' Basic Alfredo Sauce

This is a basic sauce I have been making for ages. I enjoy it over angel hair pasta

3 Onions minced
6 Cloves Garlic minced
1 Teaspoon Allspice
2 Teaspoons sugar
Olive oil
1 Lb. Parmesan cheese
1 Lb. Asigio cheese
16 oz. Heavy cream
Milk
2 Tablespoons cracked fresh pepper
2 Cans Chicken stock
2 Teaspoons dried chopped parsley

Sautee` onions and garlic in the olive oil and add the chicken stock, bring to a boil.
Add the dry spices bring to a simmer
At a very low heat add the heavy cream and stir in the cheeses.
Once simmering add milk to get to the right consistency

*Note
May be served with:
2 Lbs. Shrimp sautéed in olive oil
2 Lbs Browned in olive oil chicken breasts
2 Lbs. Cubed salmon dusted in flour and sautéed in olive oil

Dennis' Meat Sauce

I prepare this sauce at least three times per months. The family enjoys it best for a spaghetti sauce.

1½ lbs. ground round of beef
1 lb. ground pork or 1 tube breakfast sausage
1 large chopped onion
4 cloves chopped garlic
½ small chopped green bell pepper
½ small chopped red bell pepper (optional)
1 small minced carrot
2 cans tomato sauce
1 small can tomato paste
1 can chopped tomatoes
2 cans (tomato sauce) water
2 tablespoons Italian seasonings
2 tablespoons sea salt
1 teaspoon sugar
1 teaspoon black pepper
½ teaspoon crushed red pepper seeds
Olive oil
½ red wine (optional)

Brown the onion, garlic, bell peppers, and carrot in olive oil until the vegetables are tender and translucent.
Add the meats until browned.
Add the remaining ingredients and simmer for at least 4 hours on the lowest setting allowing the sauce to simmer very slow.

Lemon Butter Sauce

¼ cup lemon juice
1 (4oz) stick of cold butter
1 small skillet
Pinch of salt
Pinch of white or black pepper

Pour lemon juice in skillet and reduce on medium heat by stirring with wooden spoon until approximately 1 tbsp of liquid remains. Cut butter into 8 portions. Over very low heat stir butter sections individually into reduced lemon until completely melted and sauce has become thick and creamy.

This sauce is ideal for asparagus, cauliflower, broccoli and goes well with veal.

Lebanese Garlic Sauce (Paste)

This is a spread that is has a very strong garlic flavor. It is best used lightly over meat. I always serve it when especially barbequing chicken marinated in olive oil and oregano.

8 bulbs of garlic (clean off paper & stem)
2 cups lemon juice
2 teaspoons. salt
6 to 8 cups Puritan oil

Put in blender (NOT a food processor) and blend until smooth on medium. Add in an extremely slow stream, 3 to 4 cups of Puritan oil. Blend constantly on about medium. It should become like a thick white mayonnaise consistency. Store in refrigerator in a glass container. Serve with meats, as a seasoning in salad dressings or on pocket bread sandwiches.
This is a tricky recipe. Sometimes it "breaks". That is, it stays thin instead of the mayonnaise consistency. The flavors remain the same. If it separates in storage, just stir or blend again.

Cranberry Orange Vinaigrette Salad Dressing

I like to use this on a salad, when I'm entertaining an outdoor event.
It accompanies the sweet taste of a barbeque, or even a Polynesian feast.
This dressing can be used as a dipping sauce for raw or cooked vegetables.

1 cup Balsamic Vinegar
1 cup Water
1 cup Cranberries, fresh or frozen
1 Navel Orange, large, peeled
3 teaspoon. honey
1 tsp. Guar Gum)

Wash and peel the navel orange, break it into sections and place in the container of a high speed blender (Vita-Mix type).
Wash and clean the cranberries and add to the blender container.
Add the other ingredients, but we suggest starting with only 1 teaspoon honey until you have tasted the dressing. More honey can be added later, if desired.
Cover, and run blender at high speed until all the ingredients are smooth (about 1 minute).
Reduce the speed to slow and continue mixing until the dressing thickens.
While the dressing is thickening, taste it, and add more honey, if desired, and continue running until the dressing thickens.
Store in a bottle in the refrigerator. It will stay fresh for a few days.
Enjoy!

Dennis's French Dressing

This dressing is one of the most common dressings still used today worldwide. I use it to marinade red meat overnight before barbequing; it adds a sweet flavor to your meat.

1 cup extra virgin olive oil
¼ cup white vinegar
½ teaspoon sea salt
few grains cayenne pepper
¼ teaspoon white pepper
2 tablespoons ginger ale (optional)

Combine entire ingredients
Chill before using.

Dennis' Caesar Dressing

This is the real version of a Caesar dressing. The anchovies may be omitted, but it will not have the proper flavor. The anchovies are not a strong taste; they basically enhance the dressing with their salt content.

¾ cups of wine vinegar
¾ cups of lemon juice
1 quart. Olive oil
4 tablespoons Worcestershire sauce
1 tablespoons salt
1 tablespoons white sugar
½ tsp cracked black pepper
2 small cloves garlic (pulverized)
3 strips minced anchovies
1 medium egg yolks

In a wooden bowl, rub the lemon juice into the wood as much as possible.
Rub the garlic.
Add the anchovies and rub the entire liquid throughout the bowl add the salt
Whisk in the egg yolks, they should start to appear as if the are cooking (the acid from the juices will cook the yolks), if not keep whisking.
Add remaining ingredients and mix thoroughly

Always use fresh romaine lettuce, croutons and top with slivered Parmesan cheese. I like adding a few grape tomatoes, and very thin purple onion rings. Adding the cracked pepper from a mill adds a nice touch.

Lionel's Fast and Easy Caesar Dressing – Lionel Gemus

This recipe makes a large amount of dressing. It is from the Statler Hilton hotel in New Orleans. I would use it if I were to serve guests that were not too fond knowing that the dressing contained anchovies. (Most people do not like the taste), and pressed for time.

2 cups of wine vinegar
2 cups of lemon juice
3qts. Olive oil
½ cup Worcestershire sauce
2tbsp salt
1 ½ tsp black pepper
6 small cloves garlic (pulverized)

Mix thoroughly

You might have to adjust the quantities to suit a normal household.

Spicy Smoked Tomato

A nice not to spicy salad dressing. Pour over any salad or vegetable to spice up you meal.

2½ cups Water
1 cup Vinegar, white
1-6 oz. can Tomato Paste
1 clove Garlic, large
1 Tbsp. Oregano, dried
1 Tbsp. Basil, dried
2 Tbsp. Dill Weed, dried
1 Chipotle Pepper
½ Tsp. Guar Gum, powdered (plant-derived thickener; adjust quantity to desired consistency)

Pineapple Salsa:

I enjoy this salsa with just about everything. From tortilla chips to spooning it right out of the bowl. Best served when cold.

1 pineapple, peeled and sliced into 1/2-inch thick slices
2 red onions, peeled and sliced into 1/2-inch thick slices
3 green jalapenos
2 red jalapenos
Extra-virgin olive oil, for coating
1 tablespoon chopped mint leaves
1 tablespoon chopped Italian parsley leaves
1 lime, juiced
Salt and freshly ground black pepper

Mix together and chill

Stuffing's

If your stuffing isn't right, you meal will flop. Stuffing is very important to your guests. At the dinner table, I will eat the stuffing first and become satisfied without eating any of the remaining menu.

Dennis' Corn Bread Oyster Stuffing

My favorite stuffing. Mild in flavor, yet allowing not to overpower the delicate flavor of your favorite bird. The kids sometimes ask me to serve as a side dish.

1 lb. giblets (boil until tender, grind or chop fine)
2 cups onions, chopped fine
1½ cups celery, chopped fine
6 cups cooked corn bread, crumbled
3 cups seasoned bread crumbs (soaked in oyster water)
2 large eggs
1 teaspoons chopped garlic
3 cups chicken stock
3 heaping tablespoons ground sage
2 tablespoons butter (for sautéing)
½ cup butter (for stuffing mix)

In a skillet sauté onions, celery, bell peppers in butter until clear. Add giblets. Cook for 5 minutes. Add soaked bread crumbs and corn bread. Add eggs, chicken stock, garlic and butter. Put in casserole and bake at 350 degrees for 20-25 minutes.

Yields: 2 quarts

Corn Bread & Oyster Stuffing - Lionel Gemus

A nice alternative to the traditional corn bread stuffing. Don't allow the thought of the oysters scare you. They add a very delicate flavor.

1 lb. giblets (boil until tender, grind or chop fine)
2 cupsonions, chopped fine
1½ cups celery, chopped fine
6 cups cooked corn bread, crumbled
3 cups bread crumbs (soaked in oyster water)
3 dozen oysters (reserve oyster water)
2 medium eggs
1 teaspoons chopped garlic
2 teaspoons seafood Cajun seasoning (optional)
3 cups chicken stock

In a skillet sauté onions, celery, bell peppers until clear. Add giblets and oysters. Cook for 5 minutes. Add soaked bread crumbs and corn bread. Add eggs, chicken stock, garlic and seafood "Cajun magic". Put in casserole and bate at 350 degrees for 20-25 minutes.
Yields: 2 quarts

Dennis' Oyster Stuffing

Oyster dressing is by far my favorite. The oysters add a very nice delicate flavor, not over powering the dressing. I try to hide the ingredients when I prepare a holiday meal, I don't think the family would be very happy if they knew I have added oysters into the dressing they so much wait for.

11/2 cups margarine
2 cups celery, finely chopped
2 cups green bell pepper, finely chopped
3 cups onions, finely chopped
2 tablespoons Cajun magic seafood seasoning
1 teaspoon garlic, minced
3 bay leaves
8 oz (about 20) small to medium oysters in their liquor
1 cup (approx) bread crumbs
2 tablespoons unsalted butter, softened
1/2 cup green onions, finely chopped

Melt ¼ cup margarine in a large skillet over high heat.
Just before completely melted, add ½ cup celery, ½ cup bell pepper, and ¾ cup onions.
Sautee over high heat until the onions become dark brown (but not burned), stirring occasionally. Add 2 tsp Cajun magic and the minced garlic.
Stir and reduce heat to medium. Cook uncovered 5 minutes, stirring occasionally.
Return fire to high and cook 3 minutes. Meanwhile drain the liquor from the oysters and add enough water to the liquid to make 1 cup.
Add the oyster water to the skillet and stir. Cook 12 more minutes stirring occasionally stir in 1 tsp Cajun magic.
Add 1 cup bread crumbs or enough to have a moist but not runny dressing; turn off the fire and stir.
Stir in the drained oysters and remove dressing to a baking pan and bake 30 minutes at 350 degrees, remove the bay leaves, stir in the butter and green onions, and serve immediately.

Yield: 6 cups.

Dirty Rice Dressing

A great Cajun dressing that can be used as a side dish. I enjoy it out of the bird accompanying a juicy steak.

½ cup chopped yellow onions
½ cup chopped celery
½ cup chopped bell pepper
¼ cup green onions chopped
2 cloves chopped garlic
1 tablespoon fresh parsley chopped fine
1 teaspoon butter
½ tablespoon season salt
1 teaspoon black pepper
2 bay leaves
1 quart chicken stock (store bought is fine)
2 chicken bouillon cubes
2 cups raw white rice
1 tablespoon kitchen bouquet

from one chicken, the liver, gizzard, and heart chopped fine

In a pot, melt butter, and add the onions, celery, bell pepper, and garlic.
Cook until onions are transparent.
Add chicken parts, seasonings, and kitchen bouquet, and simmer until almost dry.
Pour in the chicken stock. Bouillon cubes, and rice, bring to a boil, reduce heat to low.
Cover and simmer very low until the rice is tender.

Seasonings

Take the time to read this section thoroughly. There are recipes that will be needed in other recipes in this book.

All Purpose Seasoning

This seasoning blend is made with thyme, nutmeg, oregano, pepper, parsley, cayenne pepper and other herbs and spices. This is an all-purpose seasoning recipe for vegetables or meat.

1 teaspoon dried leaf basil, crumbled
1 teaspoon ground mace
1 teaspoon ground cloves
1 teaspoon dried leaf thyme, crumbled
1 teaspoon ground nutmeg
1 teaspoon leaf oregano, crumbled
1 teaspoon black pepper
1 teaspoon dried parsley flakes
½ teaspoon ground cayenne pepper
1 teaspoon savory
Mix all together. You can be stored for at least one year.

Dennis' Special Seasoning

Make as much as you like. It will last for up to one year. My family sometimes uses it as they would salt and pepper. I have seen my youngest daughter Ashley sprinkle it on popcorn.

21/2 tablespoons paprika
2 tablespoons salt
2 tablespoons sugar
2 tablespoons garlic powder
1 tablespoon black pepper
1 tablespoon onion powder
1 tablespoon cayenne pepper
1 tablespoon dried leaf oregano
1 tablespoon dried thyme
½ teaspoon ground celery seed

Combine and store in an airtight jar

Dennis' Season Salt

I use this instead salt quite often. Try sprinkling on popcorn, tastes great. Recipe for seasoned salt with salt, thyme, garlic salt, onion powder, and other herbs and seasonings

6 tablespoons sea salt
½ teaspoon dried thyme leaves
½ teaspoon marjoram
½ teaspoon garlic salt or garlic powder
2¼ teaspoons paprika
¼ teaspoon curry powder
1 teaspoon dry mustard
¼ teaspoon onion powder
¼ teaspoon dill weed
½ teaspoon celery salt

Put all ingredients into a mini food processor or small blender container and blend on low.

Dennis' Blackened Seasonings

I really enjoy me steak blackened over the grill. This is a good recipe for all meats.

1 heaping tablespoon paprika
2 teaspoons salt
1 heaping teaspoon garlic powder
1 heaping teaspoon onion powder
¼ to ½ teaspoon ground cayenne pepper
2 teaspoons black pepper
½ teaspoon leaf thyme
½ teaspoon leaf oregano

Mix the ingredients well and funnel into a shaker. Seal well and store in a cool dry place.

Cajun Seasoning Blend recipe

Use it on everything, from a juicy steak to popcorn!

1 cup salt
1 cup garlic powder
1 cup onion powder
½ cup dried oregano leaves
½ cup dried sweet basil
¼ cup dried thyme leaves
¼ cup black pepper
¼ cup white pepper
¼ cup cayenne pepper
1¼ cups paprika

Combine all ingredients in a food processor and pulse until blended well. Use as a general cooking seasoning

Fish seasoning recipe

Sprinkle on your favorite fish before grilling or barbequing. Brings out the flavor of your seafood.

2 tablespoons parsley
1 tablespoon dried, powdered lemon rind
1 tablespoon celery seed
1 tablespoon savory
1 tablespoon thyme
1 tablespoon marjoram
1 teaspoon dried chives
1 crushed bay leaf

Mix all together. Will hold for over a year in an airtight container.

To make Clam or Shrimp Dip, powder 3 tablespoons Fish Seasoning Mix and add to 1 cup sour cream. Stir in 1 small can drained clams or shrimp, a little salt and Worcestershire sauce to taste.

Dennis' Hot 'N Spicy Seasonings

Use this in everything you want to have a little "kick"

1 cup paprika
6 tablespoons dried oregano, crushed
6 teaspoons chili powder
4 teaspoons garlic powder
4 teaspoons cracked black pepper
1½ teaspoon red (cayenne) pepper
1½ teaspoon dry mustard

Mix all ingredients together.
Store in an air tight container.
Lasts for at least 6 months.

Grecian Seasoning

Great on any lamb recipe. I also use it when grilling chicken.

4 tablespoons oregano
6 teaspoons ground fennel seeds
6 teaspoons dried lemon grass
¾ teaspoon black pepper

Grind all ingredients to a fine powder in a high speed coffee mill. Finely sieve into a container, then tightly seal.

Hot 'N Spicy Seasonings

Use this in everything you want to have a little kick in it.

1 cup paprika
6 tablespoons dried oregano, crushed
6 teaspoons chili powder
4 teaspoons garlic powder
4 teaspoons cracked black pepper
1½ teaspoon red (cayenne) pepper
1½ teaspoon dry mustard

Mix all ingredients together.
Store in an air tight container.
Lasts for at least 6 months

Special Seasoning

Make as much as you like. It will last for up to one year. My family sometimes uses it as they would salt and pepper. I have seen my youngest daughter Ashley sprinkle it on popcorn.

2 ½ tablespoons paprika
2 tablespoons salt
2 tablespoons sugar
2 tablespoons garlic powder
1 tablespoon black pepper
1 tablespoon onion powder
1 tablespoon cayenne pepper
1 tablespoon dried leaf oregano
1 tablespoon dried thyme
½ teaspoon ground celery seed

Combine and store in an airtight jar

Dough's

It id crucial your dough is perfect. Follow the instructions exactly as written. For baking use high gluten flour.

Basic Flaky Butter Pie Crust Dough

I find the easiest way is not to precisely measure the ingredients. When I create this dough, I find that it will always need a little adjustment. Most important, is that you want to start off with COLD water, and add a small amount at a time (My grandmother (Nana) taught me to add just a couple of tablespoons at a time). "Kneading" it as you work the dough into just a little more moist than bread or pizza dough. Remember, not to make the dough too moist, you will be rolling it out into a piecrust.

Here is how I start out:

4 cups all purpose flour
2 stick 100% butter
1 teaspoon sea salt
½ teaspoon sugar

I knead out the flour, salt, sugar, and butter together until very well mixed.
I then start adding the COLD water a very small amount at a time, kneading the dough very well in-between the adding of more COLD water, so that a good consistency can be created, to roll out into a piecrust.

Basic Pastry Dough

4 cups all-purpose flour
½ teaspoon salt
½ teaspoon pepper
1½ sticks unsalted butter or margarine
¾ cup shortening
½ to ¾ cups COLD water

In a large mixing bowl, sift together the flour, salt and pepper. Fold in butter and shortening with a pastry blender or rub between the palms of your hands until the texture becomes thoroughly mixed, but quite course. Spoon in cold water one spoon at a time (this is very important) and form two balls. If water remains, discard it; do not use all the water in not needed.
Store in plastic wrap and place in the refrigerator for at least one hour. This may be frozen until needed.

Makes 2 9 inch pie crusts.

Pastizzi Dough

Pastizzi are the most known delicacy in Maltese cuisine. They are what most non-Maltese people recognize for our vast array of meals. Cheese pastizzi in Malta are served with morning tea, while delicately "dipping" in a very small amount of sugar. Meat or cheese, are served from brunch to a midnight snack. I have had so many acquaintances approach me after finding out that I was from Maltese origin ask where they can purchase them or how to make them. Pastizzi are time consuming, and take practice, but once mastered, you will realize that this is an art in food making not just another meal.

3 cups shortening (approximately)
5 cups flour (I use only Gold Medal)
2 cups COLD water
dash of salt

Put the flour, water and salt in an electric mixer with a dough hook attachment. Mix as you would for bread dough for approximately 20 minutes or until dough ball is formed. It should feel slightly moist and as soft as a baby's behind. Cover with a moist clean towel and let sit for 1 hour. Cut about one eighth of the dough and open like pizza dough on a clean lightly greased flat surface. Spread with a rolling pin as thin as you can get it without tearing the dough. Spread a generous amount of pure vegetable shortening (I prefer Crisco). Now if you have a small wooden rod (dowel) the size of a bird cage perch, this works best. I start at one end and gently roll the edge around the dowel. I roll just a small amount of dough, and then I begin to roll, lift, and pull the dough do that it becomes thinner, but, be very careful not to rip or tear the dough. Repeat this process until you reach a roll approximately 1 ½ inches thick. Cut into 12 inch rolls and refrigerate until cool, or can be frozen.

When ready for use, cut the dough roll into one inch sections. Lay each piece on its side so that the circles are facing up, (as if it were a tree trunk, with the rings on top). Spread out with your fingers very gently, to about ¼ inch thick, starting in the center. Place around one tablespoon of filling in the center and fold over the sides and pinch in the center to seal.

Bake 1 hour at 375 degrees or until golden browned. Let stand for 15 minutes before serving.

*for filling (meat or cheese) refer to filling

Ravioli Dough

This dough can be used as ravioli or even for periogi. It is a standard dough that will allow you to either boil, or pan fry. The ingredients you choose to stuff with is up to you. Experiment.

5 cups all-purpose flour, plus more for dusting
1 teaspoon salt
6 large eggs
2 tablespoons extra-virgin olive oil

To make the pasta dough: In an electric mixer fitted with a dough hook, combine the flour and salt. Add the eggs, 1 at a time, and continue to mix. Pour in 1 tablespoon olive oil and continue to mix until a smooth dough is formed. If the dough is too dry drizzle in a bit of water, if it is too wet sprinkle in some more flour. Dust some flour on a work surface, knead and fold the dough until it is elastic and smooth, this should take about 10 minutes. Brush the surface of the dough with the remaining olive oil and wrap the dough in plastic wrap; let rest for about 30 minutes to allow the gluten to relax.

To make the dough by hand: Combine the flour and salt on a flat work surface, shape into a mound, and make a well in the center. Add the eggs and 1 tablespoon olive oil to the well and lightly beat with a fork. Gradually draw in the flour from the inside wall and mix it with the beaten eggs. Use 1 hand for mixing and the other to protect the outer wall. Continue to incorporate all the flour until it forms a smooth dough. Dust some flour on the work surface; knead and fold the dough until it is elastic and smooth, this should take about 10 minutes. Brush the surface of the dough with the remaining olive oil and wrap the dough in plastic wrap; let rest for about 30 minutes to allow the gluten to relax.

To roll out the dough: Cut the ball of dough in half, cover and reserve the piece you are not using to prevent it from drying out. Dust the counter and dough with a little flour. Press the dough into a rectangle and roll it through a pasta machine set at the widest setting 2 or 3 times. Guide the dough with your hand as it emerges from the rollers to prevent it from puncturing or stretching. Dust the sheets with extra flour whenever the dough gets sticky. Reduce the setting and crank the dough through again 2 or 3 times. Continue reducing the setting and rolling until the machine is at its narrowest setting; the dough should be paper-thin, about 1/8-inch thick for ravioli. Roll out the other half.

Roux

When it comes to a thickening agent, Roux is the best there is. Many renditions of this recipe have been used. I like to use this one that call for butter. A Roux is the basis of all of your stews, gumbos, bisques, or anything that your are doing with leftovers that requires a good, rich, brown gravy. The thickness of your gravy can always vary, according to the amount of water, stock or bouillon that you will eventually add to the basic cooked Roux mixture.

Here is the procedure for the basic Roux, and it will require approximately 20-30 minutes of your time, because you must stand watch over this, stirring religiously all the while. This may sound like trouble, but it will make or break your dish.

STEP 1

Keep warm in separate pot any water, stock or bouillon that you are eventually going to use as your liquid addictive.

STEP 2

Thoroughly mix flour and butter together in a cold pot or skillet. Place over medium heat, and start stirring, scraping all browned bits from the bottom of the pan. When it starts to turn brown, then dark brown, remove the pot from the fire immediately. Slowly incorporate your water, stock or bouillon onto the Roux, STIRRING CONSTANTLY all the time. Return to low heat and liquid needed for consistency of dish in the making. Keep in mind that vegetables give off water and will tend to thin sauce over a long period of time. It is better to keep a rather thick consistency, and toward the end of cooking then thin to desired consistency with water, stock or bouillon.

Breads and Rolls

**The aroma alone will be an invitation
Your guests will admire a chef that takes the time to serve warm
homemade bread.**

Easy Morning Rolls

Fast, easy, and full of flavor that your family will enjoy with breakfast or alone.
*You may want to prepare this the night before.

1 32 oz package frozen bread dough
1 3 oz. package "cook and serve" Vanilla pudding
1 cup crown sugar
½ cup butter
½ cup chopped pecans

Spray a bunt ban with a vegetable spray and sprinkle the pecans into the pan
Place bread roll/dough side by side in the bunt pan. Do not overlap, make one layer only.
Sprinkle dry vanilla pudding over frozen rolls. Put butter and brown sugar into a sauce pan and heat to a boil.
Pour over rolls, cover with foil and let rise overnight.
Heat in a 350 degree oven for 30 – 45 minutes or until golden brown

Maltese Bread - (Hobz)

This is very typical Maltese bread. It has a wonderful flavor when just out the oven. I like to serve it with any meal, but most of all, I like to enjoy it with a pat of butter and a chunk of any Italian cheese. Store in a plastic, but the bread will not last for more than 48 hours. Sorry the recipe asks for metric weights. But this came directly from Malta.

600g. flour
10g. salt
15g. sugar
15g. margarine
25g. yeast
345 mil. warm water
1 tablespoon milk

Mix the flour, salt and margarine
Add the yeast
Make a mixture of the warm water, sugar, and milk
Add to flour and knead the mixture well until the dough is white and elasticized
Place in a bowl, seal with plastic film and a wet dish towel, place in a warm place
For about one hour
Work the dough, cut into small pieces (50g).
Place on a baking sheet and let stand for 15 minutes
Place in oven at 350 degrees until golden brown (12-15 minutes)

Pogaca

This traditional Serbian bread has a texture unlike any other bread that I have eaten. Try it with you favorite luncheon meat, for a great sandwich.

2 eggs
1 cup low fat milk
1 tablespoon baking powder
2 cups all purpose flour

Combine milk and baking powder. Allow to sit for 10 minutes.
Add eggs, and mix well
Stir in flour and mix into a dough ball (you may need to add a little more flour)
Place on a pan and bake at 350 degrees until browned

Refrigerator Rolls

Try this with a fresh fruit jam, first thing in the morning before breakfast. What a treat in my home!

2/3 cups sugar
1 cup BOILING water
2 yeast cakes
1 teaspoon salt
1 cup Crisco shortening
2 well beaten eggs
1 cup COLD water
6 cups all purpose flour

Dissolve yeast cakes in cold water
Mix shortening and sugar together
Pour boiling water over sugar and shortening mixture
Add yeast, eggs, salt, and flour
Mix cover and refrigerate for four hours or overnight
Bake at 350 - 350 degrees for 15 – 20 minutes or until golden brown

Spoon Rolls

Quick and easy, these informal rolls are to enjoy anytime on you table.
*You may want to prepare the batter the night before

1 package active dry yeast
2 cups water (warm)
½ cup melted butter (salted)
1 egg
¼ cup sugar
4 cups all purpose flour

Dissolve yeast in water and let stand 5 minutes.
Add butter, egg, and sugar, mix well
Stir in flour.
Cover and set in the refrigerator overnight
Spoon batter onto a greased muffin pan and bake at 375 degrees for 25 – 30 minutes

I like to take 2 parts pure butter and 1 part maple syrup, and spread on the warm rolls.

Sugar Muffins

Great in the morning with breakfast or for brunch with a cup of tea.

2 cups all purpose flour
1 cup sugar
1 cup milk
1 egg
½ cup liquid cooking oil (canola, sunflower, vegetable)
1 teaspoon salt
3 teaspoons baking powder

Beat egg with a fork, add in the oil and milk, and stir together.
Add remaining ingredients and stir well.
Batter will be lumpy.
Fill each muffin pan half way and bake at 350 degrees for 20 minutes.

Yorkshire pudding

When I was a young apprentice at the Detroit Athletic Club, one of my jobs was to make the Yorkshire pudding. The first time I helped make them, I thought that I was making pudding. After coming out of the oven, I was surprised to see they were a biscuit like bread. I believe that Yorkshire pudding gives a fine steak dinner especially prime rib, the finishing touch.

2 cups sifted flour
½ teaspoon sea salt
6 eggs
2 cups milk
Beef drippings (optional, but works best with)

Sift flour and salt together
Beat eggs until light and add the sifted flour mixture and mix well
Add milk gradually and beat for 2 – 3 minutes in a mixer
Pour batter in a muffin pan
If drippings are available, only fill ½ ways; slowly pour in a small amount of the drippings (3 tablespoons)
Bake at preheated 350 degree oven until browned

Breakfast Cornbread

When my wife Robin prepares a country breakfast, the aroma of cornbread combines with bacon will wake up the heaviest sleeper.

1 cup cornmeal
1/3 cup all-purpose flour
¼ teaspoon baking soda
1 teaspoon baking powder
1 teaspoon salt
1 egg, beaten
1 cup buttermilk

Combine dry ingredients; add beaten egg and buttermilk, mixing well.
Pour into greased, heated 8-inch or 9-inch iron skillet.
Bake for 400° for 20 minutes, or until lightly browned.
Buttermilk cornbread serves 8.

Appetizers:

Always start off your gathering with appetizers. It may be few to abundant choices. Always consider serving an appetizer to start off a successful evening.

Bean Appetizer   (Bigilla)

This Maltese appetizer reminds me of Mexican refried beans. Same consistency, with a slightly different flavor. Bigilla is to be enjoyed with sliced tomatoes, onions, and crusty breads.

2 lbs. fresh pinto or fava beans (can, jarred, may be used)
6 cloves minced garlic
4 -5 sprigs fresh parsley
2 tablespoons capers
1 sm. hot pepper
¼ cup extra virgin olive oil
2 teaspoons salt and fresh ground pepper

Prepare beans as directed on package
Chill after beans have been thoroughly cooked
Add remaining ingredients and place in a food processor and grind until
a thick paste is formed
Place in a tightly capped jar and use as needed
I like to serve with a fresh loaf of Maltese bread and garden raw vegetables
drizzled with olive oil

Serve in the center of a dinner/salad plate surrounded with a thin pool of extra virgin oil and with fresh Maltese bread.

Carmel Apple Dip

This is a light summer appetizer. This can be served with a crisp white wine while having a delightful conversation amongst friends.

1 Lb. Cream cheese
2 Cups Dark brown sugar
4 Teaspoons Vanilla
8 – 12 Apples of your choice, cored and sliced into wedges

Allow cream cheese to soften, add brown sugar and vanilla
Beat in a mixer and refrigerate.
Core and slice apples and mix with a small amount of lemon juice and water to prevent apples from browning.
Serve together.

Dan's Cheesy Mushroom Caps

This recipe was passed down to me. I have never tried it, but this seems to be something that I would want to be on my appetizer table.

1 lb. ground sirloin
15 large mushroom caps
1 teaspoon sea salt
1 teaspoon cracked pepper
½ lb. pepper jack cheese
½ lb. cheddar cheese
½ lb. provolone cheese
2 teaspoons ground basil

Brown ground sirloin in a pan, while browning, wash mushroom caps.
In a bowl, shred pepper jack and cheddar cheeses (or buy them already shredded).
Add salt, Basil and black pepper and mix together.
Add cheese and spice mixture to the ground sirloin, over a low flame, allowing the cheese to melt, stirring often.
When completely melted, remove from heat.
On a baking sheet, place mushrooms caps and fill with the mixture
Slice the provolone cheese thin and add to the top and bake at 350 degrees for 10 minutes.

Dennis' Meatballs

I have never had anyone tell me these meatballs weren't fabulous. The mustard and current jelly gives it a flavor like nothing else. Once you have served this appetizer, you'll be forced to serve it again and again!

1 pound prepared Italian meatballs (frozen)
2 jars beef gravy
1 16 oz. jar yellow mustard
2 jars red current jelly or jam
2 teaspoons garlic powder
2 teaspoons dried chopped parsley
1 teaspoon cracked pepper
2 teaspoons sea salt

In a saucepan, warm all ingredients and pour over meatballs mixing well.
Bake at 350 degrees for 45 minutes.
Serve at room temp. Before serving, pierce with frilly toothpicks.

Dennis' Capunata

Capunita is a Maltese menagerie of roasted vegetables. I have seen this used as a pasta sauce, both hot and cold. I like to serve this as an appetizer with a loaf of crusty bread for dipping. A large amount can be prepared and then jarred for later use.

2 large chopped onions
5 cloves finely chopped garlic
1 large poached eggplant in 1 inch cubes
4 large ripe tomatoes or 1 large can stewed tomatoes
2 bell sliced peppers (I like to use different colors)
1 cup pitted black olives sliced thin
¼ cup extra virgin olive oil
¼ cup small capers
3 tablespoons tomato paste
Few sprigs each: oregano, basil, parsley and mint
If not available, dried may be used at 1 teaspoon each

Sautee the onions, garlic and peppers until just tender but still firm
Add the remaining ingredients and simmer for 25 – 30 minutes on very low heat
If necessary, add water to the pot to hold a small amount of broth

This dish may very well be served hot. I prefer to bring it down to room temperature. I serve it with a loaf of crusty bread. Be sure to allow enough broth, so that your guests may "dip" the bread into the broth while enjoying the vegetables.

Dennis' Spiced Ginger Shrimp

I went to a summer get together and one of the guests brought over this scrumptious dish. I could have sat in the corner and ate all these shrimps

2 Lbs. shrimp, peeled and divined
Marinade:
2/3 cups soy sauce
½ cup olive oil
2 tablespoons brown sugar
1½ teaspoons ground ginger
1 medium onion, minced
3 gloves garlic minced

Combine marinade ingredients and marinate shrimp overnight in the refrigerator

Dennis' Pickled Vidalia Onions
Basal Tal-Pikless

The Maltese community savors pickled onions. I after experimenting with several onions and different recipes, have found this one I came up with satisfies most. I use sweet Vidalia onions and sugar for a sweet pickle. My father and I would eat these as if they were apples. A loaf of bread, some fontinella cheese, a few sliced tomatoes and pickled onions made a hot summer night snack, sitting on our deck made that something that I cannot forget.

12 Small to medium Vidalia onions (smaller the better)

Marinade:
2 cups white sugar
2 cups white vinegar
1 cup apple cider vinegar
1 tablespoon dry mustard
3 tablespoons red pepper seeds
3 – 4 sliced carrots
10 cloves peeled whole cloves garlic

Peel onions and vegetables and put into a hot water bath until the water cools (15 minutes).
Take 3 cups of the water bath, re-boil and dilute the sugar, and dry mustard.
In a large glass jar, place the onions and vegetables, pour the liquid in, add the red pepper seeds and completely submerge onions using the water used for the hot water bath. Allow to set for at least one week.

Skewer shrimp and grill over direct charcoal heat for approximately 20 minutes turning every five minutes.

Falafel

I seldom go to a Middle Eastern restaurant without ordering an appetizer of falafel. This is a recipe that can also be used as a side dish with a broiled meat.

1 (15 oz.) can garbanzo beans
1 egg slightly beaten
½ teaspoon ground turmeric
2 teaspoons cilantro leaves chopped
¼ teaspoon ground cumin
¼ teaspoon ground cayenne pepper
2 cloves garlic, crushed
1 tablespoon tahini (sesame seed paste)
2 rounded tablespoons cracked wheat, soak in water for 20 minutes, and squeezed dry
Salt and fresh ground black pepper
½ cup all purpose flour
Oil, for deep frying

Put the garbanzo beans into a food processor or blender with the egg, turmeric, cilantro, cumin, cayenne pepper, garlic, tahini, and soaked cracked wheat.
Season with salt and pepper.
Blend until smooth.
Shape into balls, and dust heavily with seasoned flour.
Fry the balls in hot deep frying oil, until browned.
Drain well on a paper towel and serve hot.

Linda's Sweet Fruit–Cheese Dip

I first tasted this dip at my annual Christmas party. I hesitated knowing that Khalua was used in this recipe. I didn't think that it would blend well with fruits and cheeses. This dip goes exceptionally well with strong cheeses such as sharps and smoked cheeses. Any kind of melons, apples, pears, and grapes go great.

8oz. Philadelphia cream cheese softened
8oz. sour cream
8oz. whip cream
½ cup coffee liquor
¾ cup brown sugar

Whip together until stiff.
Chill for 1 hour before serving.

Dennis' Mussels in their Shells with Garlic Butter

This is another WOW factor. It will impress your guests that enjoy the flavors of shellfish as an appetizer. Very delicate, yet this recipe has the hint of garlic.

20 mussels
1¼ cups water
½ medium onion, sliced
A few sprigs of curly parsley
1 bay leaf
4 teaspoons butter (salted)
3 cloves crushed garlic
1 teaspoon parsley, minced
Salt and freshly ground black pepper
1 teaspoons Italian bread crumbs
2 teaspoons finely grated Gruyere cheese

Tap the mussel on a flat surface and discard any that remain open (they are already dead and can be poisonous).
Scrub the remaining and place in a large pot with salted water, onion, parsley sprigs, and bay leaf.
Cover and simmer for 2 minutes, shaking the pan occasionally until the mussels have opened.
Strain and again, discard any mussels that have not opened.
Remove the top half of each shell.
Soften the butter, and beat in the parsley, garlic and season with salt and pepper.
Mix the bread crumbs and cheeses together.
Just before serving, preheat the broiler to 400 degrees.
Place a dab of garlic butter on each mussel, and sprinkle with the toppings.
Broil until browned.
Serve warm with slices of hard crust baguettes'.

Open Faced Tomato and Tuna Fish Sandwich
Hobz Biz-Zejt U Tun

This is one of the most traditional Maltese appetizers/snacks. I have enjoyed this as a lunchtime meal, a midnight snack and while fishing on the boat. My daughters are hooked on this snack, and now their friends are always asking for a "Maltese" sandwich.

1 loaf crusty Italian ciabatta bread
1 small can tomato paste
½ cup extra virgin olive oil
1 can tuna fish packed in oil
Sea salt & pepper
Green onions

This is an art to prepare, follow exactly as written.
Bake the bread in a 450 degree over for five minutes, or until the crust is crunchy.

Place the oil in a large shallow dish, salt and pepper
Cut the bread into thick slices
Dip the bread flat in the oil allowing it to cover the bread, but NOT saturating it
Spread the tomato paste on the bread as if it were butter
Also spread the tuna fish on the bread
Salt and pepper

Serve with green onions, capers, green olives, cucumbers and Italian cheese.

Potatoes with oil and Parsley Appetizer
(Patata Bit-Tursin U Zejt)

Very easy and can be served hot, or cold. My family always served this Maltese side dish with crispy fried fish.

6 -8 red potatoes
2 bunches parsley
2 teaspoons garlic powder
Sea salt and pepper
Extra virgin olive oil

Boil potatoes until done but not to wear the will crumble.
Slice and carefully not to break the slices, fold in chopped parsley and olive oil.
Sprinkle with garlic powder, salt and pepper to taste.

Steak Tartar

I know most guests would be afraid of consuming raw meats. But, if this meat is very fresh and grinded exactly the way the recipe calls for. It should be safe.

½ lb. filet mignon or rump steak
2 teaspoons extra virgin oil
2 raw egg yolks
1 small red onion, minced very fine
Salt and freshly ground pepper
Worcestershire sauce
20 capers
20 thin slices French baguette

Trim the steak of all fat if any.
Freeze then grind.
Refreeze then grind again two or three times to a very smooth consistency.
Beat in the oil, egg yolks, onion, and parsley, season with salt and pepper, and Worcestershire sauce.
Place a spoonful of steak tartar on top of each bread baguette and garnish with a caper.
Serve chilled.

Stuffed Mushroom Caps - Ruth Gemus

An appetizer everyone will enjoy. I always serve this recipe at my home. Your guests will appreciate the effort you took to make there experience a good one.

Sauté 2 small onions chopped fine in 2 tbsp butter for 5 minutes,
Add, ½ teaspoon Salt, Stems from 2 dry mushroom caps, chopped fine,4 Slices of bacon crisp and crumbled.
Sautee 2 minutes more.

Add:
2 tablespoons Water
1 tablespoon Worcestershire sauce

Separately and at the same time:
Sautee in 3 tablespoons butter
2 dozen mushroom caps lightly sprinkled with salt.
The caps are best if fried face down first, then face up, about 3 minutes each side.
Fill with onion and bacon mixture.

Supposed to be best piping hot, but actually are delicious cold.

"

Outdoor Barbequing and Smoking

These recipes are what I entitle
"Damn good Bar B Que

Boston Baked Beans

When entertaining an outdoor barbeque, baked beans is a must. This is a nice recipe that everyone can enjoy.

2 lb. dried navy beans
2 qt. cold water
1 medium onion, sliced
1 tablespoon salt
4 teaspoon cider vinegar
1 teaspoon prepared mustard
2 tablespoon brown sugar
½ cup molasses
¼ cup tomato ketchup
1/16 teaspoon black pepper
Hot water if needed
½ lb. salt pork, sliced or sliced bacon

Pick over and wash beans thoroughly. Add cold water, cover, heat to boiling and simmer for 30 minutes.
Drain but do not discard the liquid.
Place onion slices in bottom of a bean pot or a 10-cup casserole. (I usually use my big roaster, because it is thick enough to hold the heat evenly). Combine the next 7 ingredients and turn into the bean pot.
Add the bean and enough hot drained liquid or water to cover (about 2-1/2 cups). Arrange salt pork slices on top, cover and place in a smoker for 12- 14 hours keeping an eye on it so that they will not dry up.
 or bake in a very slow oven (250 degrees) 7-8 hours, remove cups of beans and bash.
Then stir into the remaining beans carefully.
Cover and continue to bake.
Add additional hot bean liquid or water as needed. Beans should be just covered with thick, luscious liquid.
Remove the cover 1 hour before end of cooking time to allow salt pork to brown.

10-12 servings for meal, or enough for 20 people for a smorgasbord.

Heat may be added by adding crushed red pepper to your desired flavor.

Apple Cider-Cured Smoked Salmon

If you desire to serve a seafood recipe that will impress everyone, here is it. Salmon has a delicate flavor. The smoking adds essence that will enhance your meal. Serve this with steamed vegetables, to allow the accent to be the salmon

1 cup brown sugar
1/4 cup salt
4 cups apple cider or juice
2 cinnamon sticks
1 teaspoon fennel seeds
1 teaspoon whole allspice
1 teaspoon black peppercorns
1 bay leaf
1 teaspoon red pepper flakes
6 sprigs thyme or 1/2 teaspoon dried thyme

1 large salmon fillets (about 1 pound each), skin and pin bones removed
a small bundle of wood chips or chunks

To make the brine: In a saucepan, combine the brown sugar, salt, and apple juice and bring to a boil. Add the remaining brine ingredients, remove from the heat, and cool. This brine can be made 2 to 3 days in advance and kept in the refrigerator.

Submerge the salmon fillets in the liquid brine for at least 6 hours or overnight, refrigerated. Remove the salmon from the brine and place, uncovered, on a wire rack set in a sheet pan. Refrigerate the fillets for at least 6 hours, or overnight, to dry them out. (A dry fillet will take on smoke quicker than a moist fillet)

To smoke the salmon: In an outdoor grill, make a small fire using mesquite charcoal or briquettes. Once the fire has burned down to a hot bed of coals, after about 1 hour, place the soaked wood on the coals. Position the grate 8 to 12 inches above the smoking wood and place the salmon fillets on the grate.

Cover the grill and shut any open-air vents.
After 5 minutes, check the heat of the grill; large fillets will be cooked and smoked through in approximately 30 minutes if the heat is low, about 300 to 350 degrees , while a hotter fire will cook the fillets in 15 to 20 minutes.
Serve the salmon hot off the grill.

Dennis' Barbequed Country Pork Ribs

Most people prefer baby back ribs. I for one think that country ribs have much more flavor. Sometimes a cut of meat which has very little fat that is being used for barbequing tend to lose flavor, it dries out and become rather tough. A fatter cut of meat, will self baste on a barbeque grill adding the flavor. Don't be frightened of the fat, most of it will melt away in the grill.

4 lbs. country ribs
Garlic Powder
Onion Powder
Spanish Paprika
Black Pepper
Olive Oil
Brown Sugar
Seasoning Salt
Japanese Hosing Sauce (Purchased in a Japanese Market)
Dennis' Dark Bar-B-Queue Sauce

Skin and wash ribs, pat dry.
Lay bone side down on a baking rack, Spray vegetable spray on each side, and sprinkle on the following spices:
  Garlic Powder
  Onion Powder
  Paprika
  Black Pepper
Place on a hot Grill and slow cook for 20 minutes on each side.
Turn on the sides and sprinkle with the following spices:
  Brown Sugar
  Seasoning Salt
Brush both sides with half homemade dark bar-b-queue sauce and half Japanese hosing sauce, while turning every five minutes.
Cook until medium well.

Dennis' Chicken or Beef Fajitas

On one summer weekend, I make it an effort to invite friends and family over for a Mexican Fiesta. I start of with fresh sangria, moving to the main course of chicken and or beef fajitas, rice and refried beans. Finishing the evening with flan and margarita cocktails.

1½ pounds boneless, skinless chicken breasts
2 tablespoons olive oil
3 tablespoons lime juice
2 cloves garlic
1 cup packed cilantro leaves
½ jalapeno, seeded
Salt and pepper
1 tablespoon olive oil
1 large onion, peeled and cut into 1/2 inch slices
1 green bell pepper, seeded and sliced
2 tablespoons olive oil
3 potatoes, cut into 1/2 inch cubes
Salt and pepper
Cayenne pepper
10 flour tortillas

Flatten chicken breasts to 1/2 inch thickness between two sheets of plastic wrap with a mallet or rolling pin.
Place chicken breasts in glass baking dish. In a blender combine oil, lime juice, garlic, cilantro, jalapeno and salt and pepper.
Blend until smooth and pour over chicken.
Cover with plastic wrap and let chicken marinate for 30 minutes.
In a large skillet over medium setting heat oil.
Add onions and peppers and cook until they are tender and begin to brown.
In a 9x13 glass baking dish toss potatoes with oil and seasonings.
Bake in a 375 degree oven until crispy, about 30 minutes.
Stir occasionally to prevent sticking.
Heat a cast iron grill pan or an outdoor grill.
Toast flour tortillas for about 30 seconds per side and keep warm in an aluminum foil pocket.
Grill the chicken on each side for 4-5 minutes.
To serve, slice chicken into even strips. Serve hot with onions and peppers, grated jack cheese, salsa and sour cream.

Dennis' Sesame Barbequed Steaks

This is one of my favorite ways to cook a New York strip steak, on the grill. This recipe calls for Japanese Hosin sauce. It is wonderful flavor, adding a sweet taste, combined with the toasted sesame, created in the back of your palette. It is light, yet, full of flavor, where a traditional barbeque sauce may be a little too strong. I sometimes prepare the steaks the night before and take them out 2 to 3 hours before grilling, to allow them to breathe and reach room temperature, this procedure will create a stronger pungent flavor, for some it may be a little to strong.

4 New York strip steaks ½ inch thick
½ cup toasted sesame oil
¼ cup soy sauce
2 teaspoons garlic powder
2 teaspoons onion powder
1 teaspoon black pepper
2 teaspoons Spanish paprika
seasoned rice vinegar
Japanese Hosin sauce

Line up steaks in a row with wax paper underneath them and rub in the following:

Toasted sesame oil, Garlic powder, Onion powder, Soy sauce, Black pepper, And Spanish Paprika.
Wrap tightly and let stand in the refrigerator for 1 to 2 hours.
Place on a hot grill and slow cook for 7 minutes on each side.
Brush a thin coat of 2 parts Japanese Hosin' sauce to 1 part seasoned rice vinegar.
Cook for an additional 2 minutes on each side or until done to preference.
Sprinkle with sesame seeds after removing from the grill.

A nice condiment is Japanese hosing sauce with a few drops of Tabasco sauce for dipping.

Dennis' Smoked Portobello Mushrooms

Absolutely my favorite way to serve mushrooms, especially for an outdoor event.

Olive oil, for sautéing
6 cloves garlic, chopped
2 cup chopped onion
1½ cups chopped carrots
1½ cups chopped celery
3 pound smoked Portobello mushrooms
1½ pounds white button mushrooms, sliced
½ cup dry sherry
4 cups chicken stock
4 cups heavy cream
6 sprigs fresh thyme, leaves chopped
Salt and freshly ground black pepper

Place the mushrooms in a smoker and heavy smoke with hickory wood for one hour.
In a large sauté pan over medium high heat add olive oil to coat.
Add garlic, onion, carrots and celery and sauté until onions are translucent.
Add Portobello's and button mushrooms and sauté until tender, about 10 minutes.
Add dry sherry to deglaze and bring to a simmer for 5 minutes.
Then add chicken stock, heavy cream and thyme.
Bring back to a simmer for until desired consistency is reached.
Add salt and pepper to taste.

Dennis' Whiskey Steak Marinade

A great way to impress your dinner guests. The whiskey gives the meat such a distinct flavor like no other. Sweet, yet tangy, spicy, yet pungent.

1 cup whiskey
1 cup pineapple juice
6 tablespoons tomato paste
¾ cup dark molasses
2/3 cup applesauce
1 cup brown sugar, unpacked
1 cup raisins
4 teaspoon lemon zest
Pinch cayenne pepper
4 rib eye steaks

Salsa, as accompaniment

In a large bowl, whisk together the whiskey, pineapple juice, tomato paste, molasses, applesauce, brown sugar, raisins, lemon zest, and cayenne pepper. Then, add the steaks to the bowl and let it marinate for 30 to 40 minutes in the refrigerator.
Preheat an outdoor grill. Place the steak on the grill and cook until desired internal temperature. Serve with your favorite salsa.

More meat can be marinated. This recipe can be stored in a jar for up to 1 month.

Dennis' Grilled Scallops with Pineapple Salsa

As good as the title. Exquisite for an outdoor affair. Your friends will never forget this recipe. This marinate adds a sweet flavor, yet a hint of mint infuses the scallops perfectly.

15 large sea scallops
1 tablespoon chopped mint leaves
1 teaspoon chopped rosemary leaves
Extra-virgin olive oil
Freshly ground black pepper
Kosher salt
Teriyaki or barbecue sauce, optional
Pineapple salsa, recipe follows
Soak wooden skewers in water for 30 minutes.

Place the scallops on paper towels to blot dry.
Thread 2 skewers through 5 scallops. Repeat 2 more times.
Sprinkle mint and rosemary over the scallops and drizzle extra-virgin olive oil generously over the skewered scallops.
Grind black pepper over the skewered scallops also drizzle more olive oil over top and refrigerate for 30 minutes.
Season scallops with salt.
Oil a hot grill and place the skewers over high heat for about 2 minutes on each side.
At this point, you may brush on teriyaki or your favorite barbecue sauce. Serve immediately over pineapple salsa.

Pineapple Salsa:
1 pineapple, peeled and sliced into 1/2-inch thick slices
2 red onions, peeled and sliced into 1/2-inch thick slices
3 green jalapenos
2 red jalapenos
Extra-virgin olive oil, for coating
1 tablespoon chopped mint leaves
1 tablespoon chopped Italian parsley leaves
1 lime, juiced

Salt and freshly ground black pepper
Oil your grill. Place pineapple slices onto hot grill for 4 minutes on each side. Gently toss the onion slices and jalapenos in olive oil. Place onto the hot grill for 3 to 4 minutes on each side. Remove from grill. Peel skin off of jalapenos. Cube the pineapple, removing the inner core. Cube the onion and mince the jalapenos. Combine all of them with the chopped herbs in a large bowl. Add lime juice and drizzle with olive oil. Season with salt and freshly ground black pepper, to taste.

Robin's Barbecue Beef Short Ribs

I prefer short ribs over more expensive cuts of beef. To have a plate of these delicious ribs placed in front of me is, as if I went to heaven. This is one of Robin's best recipes. Perfect flavors accent the meat, sweet, tangy, and tart yet not overpowering.

8 pounds beef short ribs, cut across the bone
2 garlic cloves
1 bay leaf
1 cup brown mustard
½ cup red wine vinegar
1/3 cup brown sugar
2 tablespoons tomato paste
1 teaspoon cayenne pepper
3 tablespoons butter, melted
1 tablespoon molasses
3 tablespoons Worcestershire sauce
1 tablespoon granulated onion
1 tablespoon granulated garlic
Salt and pepper, to taste

Fill a large stockpot with water and bring to a boil.
Add the ribs, garlic cloves and bay leaf. Parboil the ribs, covered, for 45 minutes to 1 hour, until fork tender.
In a medium saucepan, combine all ingredients.
Pour 1 cup of the rib water into the mixture.
Cook over medium heat, stirring occasionally, for approximately 15 minutes until the sauce has thickened and is heated through.
Add the ribs to the pot, turning with tongs to coat well.
Season with salt and pepper.
Transfer the ribs to a hot outdoor grill, meat side down first, and cook 8 to 10 minutes on each side, taking care not to burn them.
Serve with remaining sauce on the side.

Tom's Tea Smoked Chicken

A delicate smoked flavored chicken. This is a common Szechwan meal, where this was the only way to cook a meal.

3 pound whole chicken
1 teaspoon ground Szechwan peppercorn
1 tablespoon salt
1 teaspoon five spice powder

Smoking Mixture:
½ cup black tea leaves
½ cup brown sugar
½ cup raw rice
2 to 3 chunks fresh ginger
2 to 3 large strips of orange zest
2 tablespoons sesame oil
Scallion brushes

Wash the chicken and pat dry inside and out with paper towels.
Combine Szechwan peppercorns, salt, and five spice powder in a small bowl. Rub the seasonings into the outside and inside cavity of the bird. Place the chicken in a large bowl, cover, and refrigerate 8 hours or overnight. Fill the lower part of a steamer with enough water to come within an inch of the cooking rack and bring the water to a rolling boil, place the chicken on the rack, and cover the steamer, steam the chicken for 45 minutes, keeping the water at a boil and replenishing it as it boils away.
 Line a large wok or a heavy Dutch oven with tight fitting lid with heavy duty aluminum foil, combine the smoking mixture ingredients and spread over the foil in the bottom of the pot and turn the heat under the pot to high and place a rack about 3 inches above the smoking mixture so that the chicken does not touch it.
Place the chicken on the rack, breast side up.
Line the inside of the lid with more foil, leaving an excess of 3 inches around the lid, cover the pot tightly and crimp the foil down so the lid fits securely and smoke doesn't escape, after you detect smoke, smoke the chicken for 20 to 25 minutes.
Turn off the heat and let the smoke subside, about 5 minutes.
The chicken should be a rich, golden brown on the outside.
Lift out the smoked chicken and transfer to a cutting board.
Immediately brush the sesame oil lightly over the outside.
Allow chicken to cool, about 10 minutes.
To serve, cut off the wings and legs.
Divide the body of the chicken in half lengthwise by cutting through the breast and backbone, lay the halves flat on the cutting board, skin side up, and use a cleaver to chop through each half, bones and all, into 3 to 4 equal pieces.
Chop the wings and legs into pieces as well.

Arrange the chicken pieces on a large platter, and garnish with the scallion brushes.

Tom's Smoked Beef Brisket

This recipe belongs to my good buddy Tom "dillbilly" Dill. After watching a few cooking shows on television, he embarked on what would be a good recipe for smoked meats. I personally think that this is one of the best smoke meat recipes I have ever tasted. The outmost important procedures in smoking meats I have learned from Tom, is that you MUST treat the meats gently as you would a newborn child. Tending to it *ALL* day. When turning and basting, be ever so careful, not to disturb the "bark" of the meat (The bark is the crust produced by the spices of the rub burning from the heat and grease released from the meat). TAKE YOUR TIME! I have realized, the more patience, the better the turnout.

1 8 to 12 Lb. beef brisket
1 jar grey Poupon mustard
1 recipe dry rub
1 recipe wet mop
Favorite Recipe for Barbeque Sauce(s)

PROCEDURE
Turn on and prepare your smoker (We use electric wet smokers)
Clean and pat dry meat. Message meat with a generous portion of dry rub. Gently not to disturb the dry rub, hand rub with Mustard throughout the meat. Sprinkle, heavily with drier rub to form a moist but firm thick coating. (This is where the bark is formed).
Place in HOT smoker fat side up, and cook undisturbed, for one hour.
Add 4 –5 five pieces water soaked *wood chips, (We both agreed, hickory works best on beef and pork), constantly feeding chips for a continuous, smoke. (approx. every 30-45 minutes), also, heavily mist with the wet mop (I use a plastic
spray bottle), every 30 minutes depending on weather, the warmer the outside temp., the more spray mopping needed, to maintain a moist, warm undisturbed, smoking procedure.
After four hours, flip meat ONE time, being VERY careful not to disturb the bark. Smoke for an additional 3 hours.
Remove meat very careful, and double wrap in heavy aluminum foil, Place Back into smoker and cook without any more wood chips for 1 ½ hours.
Remove and let stand for at least 1 hour or until meat is cool enough to handle by hand.
Pull apart by using two forks, piercing into the meat in the center and pulling Back to shred. If preferred, Brisket may be sliced very thin, but will not yield as much as when the meat has been pulled. Top with your favorite barbeque sauce(s)

*Any variety of wood chips may be used.

Tom's Smoked Pulled Pork Butt

I finally succeeded in creating a tender cut of smoked meat. At my annual Fourth of July party, my guests look forward to pulled pork with all the trimmings. The biggest secret to this recipe is treating this piece of meat as you would a baby. Be very careful when turning the meat not to disturb the bark. The slower, the better, has been a proven fact in this procedure.

3 - 6 to 10 lb. pork butts (untrimmed)
1 jar honey mustard
1 recipe dry rub
1 recipe wet mop

Recipe for your favorite barbeque sauce(s)

Preparation:
Turn on and prepare your smoker (We use electric wet smokers)
Clean and pat dry meat. Message meat with a generous portion of dry rub.
Gently not to disturb the dry rub, hand rub with Mustard throughout the meat.
Sprinkle, heavily with drier rub to form a moist but firm thick coating.
Place in a HOT smoker fat side up, and cook undisturbed, for one hour.
Add 4 –5 five pieces water soaked *wood chips, (We both agreed, hickory works best on beef and pork), constantly feeding chips for a continuous, smoke. (approx. every 30-45 minutes), also, heavily mist with the wet mop (I use a plastic
spray bottle), every 30 minutes depending on weather, the warmer the outside temp., the more spray mopping needed, to maintain a moist, warm undisturbed, smoking procedure.
After four hours, flip meat ONE time, being VERY careful not to disturb the bark. Smoke an additional 3 hours.
Remove meat very careful, and double wrap in heavy aluminum foil, Place Back into smoker and cook without any more wood chips for 1 ½ hours.
Remove and let stand for at least 1 hour or until meat is cool enough to handle by hand.
Pull apart by using two forks, piercing into the meat in the center and pulling Back to shred. Top off with your favorite barbeque sauce.

*Any variety of wood chips may be used.

Corn Grilled in the Husk

A nice presentation. I always preferred to have my corn on the grill wile still in the husk. This is a nice presentation that allows indoor roasting as a starter. If you are pressed for time, is it possible to roast the corn in the oven the day before.

12 ears fresh corn, in the husk
1½ cups mayonnaise
1½ cups freshly grated Parmigianino - Reggiano
Cayenne pepper
Lime wedges, for serving

Preheat the oven to 350 degrees or barbeque grill to medium flame.
Place the corn, still in its husks, directly on the rack and roast for about 20 minutes until the corn is soft when you press on it.
Take the corn out and let it cool a little until you can handle it, or until you're ready to serve.
When you're ready to eat, place a large grill pan on 2 burners over medium-high heat or preheat an outdoor gas or charcoal barbecue and get it very hot.
Take a few paper towels and fold them several times to make a thick square.
Blot a small amount of oil on the paper towel, and then carefully and quickly wipe the hot grates of the grill to make a nonstick grilling surface.
When the grill or grill pan is hot, peel down the husks from the roasted corn and pull out the corn silk.
Tie the husks in a knot so you can hold on to the knot like a handle and char the corn on the grill or grill pan, turning, until the kernels are slightly blackened all around and start popping, about 6 minutes.
Brush the corn with mayonnaise, and sprinkle with the Parmigianino and a little cayenne pepper so it's nicely coated. Serve with lime wedges.

Light Meals

Between mealtime snacks, should always be light and refreshing

Cuban Sandwich

If you have never tried a Cuban sandwich, you don't know what you're missing. I had the best one down while visiting Miami Florida 1988. It was from an old lady selling them on a roadside sandwich stand. The time and effort is well worth the result. I think this recipe is closest to the sandwich I had in Florida. Remember: This is a meal, I serve it with fried Plantains

½ cup mayonnaise
4 canned chipotle chiles in adobo
6 long sandwich rolls, split in half - French loaf style bread
6 thin slices Black Forest ham
12 thin slices imported Swiss cheese
2 kosher dill pickles, thinly sliced lengthwise
1½ pounds Roast Pork, thinly sliced or shredded (about 3 cups), plus reserved pan juices, (recipe follows) Kosher salt.

In a mini food processor, combine the mayonnaise and chipotles and process until smooth.
Spread the cut sides of the rolls with the chipotle mayonnaise.
Assemble the sandwiches with the ham, cheese, pickles and roast pork.
Top the meat with a spoonful of the pork pan juices and season with salt.
Close the sandwiches and tuck in any overhanging filling.
Using an electric sandwich grill press, grill the sandwiches in batches until crispy and hot. (I used a frying pan and placed another slightly smaller on top).
Alternately, preheat the oven to 325 degrees.
Set a large skillet or griddle over moderately low heat.
Arrange the sandwiches on the griddle and cover with a large baking sheet weighed down with a heavy skillet. Cook the sandwiches, turning once, until they're crisp on the outside, about 6 minutes.
Transfer the sandwiches to a baking sheet and bake until the cheese is melted, about 8 minutes.
Cut the sandwiches in half and serve immediately; pass the remaining pan juices separately.

(Continued)
For the Roast Pork:
1 (8-pound) pork shoulder, boned
1 1/2 tablespoons minced garlic
1 cup plus 2 tablespoons distilled white vinegar
¾ cup fresh lime juice
¼ cup fresh grapefruit juice
¼ cup fresh orange juice
2 tablespoons dried oregano, crumbled
1 tablespoon freshly ground black pepper
2 teaspoons adobo-style seasoning
Kosher salt and freshly ground black pepper
1 large green bell pepper, coarsely chopped
1 medium onion, coarsely chopped

Using a small, sharp knife, make 1-inch-long slashes in the skin of the pork
shoulder, about 2 inches apart. Rub the garlic into the slashes and along the
underside of the pork.
In a large glass or ceramic bowl, combine the vinegar, lime juice, grapefruit juice,
orange juice, oregano, pepper, adobo seasoning, and salt and pepper.
Stir in the green pepper and onion, then add the pork, skin side up.
Refrigerate overnight turning the meat once or twice.
Bring to room temperature before cooking.
Preheat the oven to 400 degrees.
Transfer the pork and its marinade to a roasting pan.
Cover with foil and roast until very tender, about 3 hours.
Let cool in the liquid and transfer the pork to a cutting board and discard the skin
and fat. Strain the pan juices into a glass measure and skim off the fat.
Slice or shred the pork, as desired.

*Note: The pork can be refrigerated for up to 3 days

Adobo can be purchased at most Latin grocery stores

Dennis' Spaghetti Omelets - Tarja

As a young man, my grandmother would prepare these omelets when she made spaghetti, the previous day there were an abundance of leftover cooked spaghetti. I could not wait, very light but filling. I have seen her add just a touch of a basic tomato sauce on top. Now I serve it all the time. I have tweaked it into my own recipe, giving it an American flair, adding bacon to bring out more flavor, for the rest of the family to enjoy.

1½ lbs. Angel hair pasta (boiled al dente`)
4 -6 eggs
1 lb. cooked bacon cut up (Save the bacon grease)
½ cup dried chopped parsley
½ cup parmesan cheese
1 - 2 cups grated cheddar cheese
1 teaspoon garlic powder
1 teaspoon salt
1 teaspoon cracked pepper

Mix all ingredients in a bowl, except the cheddar cheese
In a frying pan, place a small amount of olive oil, and bacon grease or just bacon grease and fry until brown on bottom, flip and brown again. Top with grated cheddar cheese

Serve with hard crust bread

French Tourtiere (QUEBEC) – Lionel Gemus

Tourtiere is a French meat pie. I have not tried this recipe just yet, but my friend Mike Gemus explained that was one of his favorite recipes his father made. Again I have left the format alone. I think it will make the recipe easier to follow.

THE PASTRY:
3 cups all purpose flour
¾ stick unsalted butter
Cut into pieces
4 tablespoons vegetable shortening

Mix in food processor w/steel knife (or in bowl with hand pastry blender) until mixture becomes the consistency of oatmeal.

ALL THE ABOVE SHOULD BE COLD

Transfer mixture to bowl, combine 10 tbsp ice water and mix with spatula or pastry blender. Transfer dough to hard surface and with the heel of your hand smear small portions of the dough to provide the final blend of fat and flour.

Gather all the dough and knead it into a smooth round ball, then separate it into two balls, one smaller than the other, the larger one being for the bottom shell.

1-10" pie plate, greased.
(This is the French flan
Pie plate, the sides are
1-3/4" high. If you use
Smaller pie plates, all
The ingredients should
Be reduced accordingly.)

roll larger ball on floured surface to approximately 13" diameter, 1/8" thick. This is very rich dough, so as you roll, on 2 or 3 occasions lift up the dough and lightly flour the surface to avoid sticking. Also sprinkle a small amount of flour on top.

When the proper size and thickness, roll the dough around the roller and unravel it over the pie pan. Lift up the sides and carefully tuck the dough upright along the inner edges. Trim the dough at the very top edge with a sharp knife.

(Continued)

2 egg whites

with soft brush cover the dough with egg white which has been beaten until frothy. This will help avoid liquids from the meat contents penetrating the dough, making it soggy. Place in refrigerator until further use.

THE MEAT FILLING:

2 lb. lean ground pork
2 cups finely chopped onion
2 green onions with the green stems finely chopped
1 large stalk celery, finely chopped Including leaves
3 cloves of garlic, minced
1 teaspoon savory
½ teaspoon ground cloves
1 teaspoon cinnamon

¾ teaspoon salt
¾ teaspoon fresh ground pepper
1 cup water
1 ½ cups stale bread crumbs

place all ingredients in fairly large pot. Mix well, bring to a boil and simmer, stirring occasionally, for 20 minutes or until quite thick and liquid is no longer apparent. If the meat is fat, it is best to put it, after cooking, into a strainer and drain off the fat.

THE FINISH:

Pre-heat oven to 400 degrees

Taste to correct any seasonings. Pour the pork mixture into the pie shell. Roll out the smaller ball of dough. Brush edges of bottom shell with water, cover with remaining dough and press the top edge lightly with palm of hands, smooth off excess.

Make openings in top crust for steam to escape when cooking. Decorate top with left over dough shapes. Brush surface with egg white for color and glossy finish.

Bake for 30 minutes or until golden In a preheated oven(400 degrees) on center grid.

Jibarito – Puerto Rican Sandwich

Authentic Puerto Rican sandwich that I can't get enough of. Wonderful because there is NO bread involved!

2 cups vegetable oil for frying
1 green plantain, peeled and halved lengthwise
2 tablespoons vegetable oil
1 clove garlic, minced
4 ounces beef skirt steak, cut into thin strips
¼ medium yellow onion, thinly sliced
1 pinch cumin
1 pinch dried oregano
1 tablespoon mayonnaise
1 slice processed American cheese, cut in half
2 slices tomato
3 leaves lettuce

Heat 2 cups vegetable oil in a large, deep skillet or deep fryer to 350 degrees F. Place plantain halves in the oil and cook 1 to 2 minutes, until they float. Remove from oil and drain on paper towels.

Place plantain halves between 2 cutting boards. Press to flatten. Place the flattened plantains back in the oil and cook for 2-3 minutes, until golden brown. Drain on paper towels.

Heat 2 tablespoons of oil in a large skillet. Add the garlic, skirt steak, onion, cumin and oregano. Cook, stirring frequently, until steak is cooked through.

To serve, spread mayonnaise on one of the plantain slices. Top with cheese, steak and onion mixture, lettuce, and tomato. Place the other plantain half on top to form a sandwich. Cut in half and serve!

Maltese Cheesecakes (Pastizzi) - Pastizzi Tal L-Irokotta

These particular pastizzi are the most popular. An ultra flaky crust surrounding a delicate ricotta cheese filling. Cheese pastizzi can be served in the A.M. for breakfast, to midnight snacks. Sometimes a sprinkle of sugar on them would create a semi-sweet dessert.

*Pastizzi Dough

Filling:
2 lbs. ricotta cheese (fresh)
2 large eggs
1 teaspoon parsley
1 tablespoon Parmesan cheese
½ teaspoon each, salt and pepper

Mix all together is a bowl, do not mix so well that it becomes pudding like. This filling should be course.

Fill according to the pastizzi dough instructions.

Meat Pastizzi - Pastizzi Tal-Laham

There is nothing better than a few pastizzi and a cold drink. My family can't wait until I place a few dozen in the oven. It is definitely a favorite food in our home. I have never met anyone that doesn't enjoy pastizzi. A great snack to a light meal, a must try.

*Pastizzi dough

Filling:
1 lb. ground beef
1 can corned beef
1 large onion chopped
2 cans drained sweet peas or
2 cups frozen sweet peas (I prefer frozen)
2 tablespoons Parmesan Cheese
2 tablespoons tomato paste
½ teaspoon each of salt, pepper and curry powder (Optional)

Brown beef, onion in olive oil and add the remaining ingredients, except fro the peas if they are canned, otherwise add all. Simmer for 30 minutes and add canned peas and cool completely. Follow pastizzi dough instructions on making a pastizzi.

Mexican Telera Sandwich

 Try these fabulous flavorful sandwiches and serve them at your party for a real delight. I tried these at a local Mexican deli in Southwest Detroit. Wow, I would never get tired of having one of these everyday in my lunchbox.

1 cup mayonnaise
2 canned chipotle chilies in adobo sauce
4 Mexican-style soft rolls (called Telera), split in half (see note)
Grilled Chicken, recipe follows
4 plum tomatoes, cut into 20 thin slices
1 Hass avocado, peeled, seeded, and cut into 16 thin slices
8 thin slices pepper Jack cheese (about 8 ounces)
Preheat oven to 350 degrees F.

Place the mayonnaise and chipotle chilies in a food processor and blend until smooth. Generously spread the cut sides of the rolls with the chipotle mayonnaise. Cover the bottom half of each roll with 1 thinly sliced chicken breast, overlapping the slices. Top each portion of chicken with 5 slices of tomato and 4 slices of avocado. Cover with 2 slices of cheese.

Place assembled sandwiches open faced on a sheet pan and bake until cheese is melted, about 8 minutes. Cover the sandwiches, slice in half and serve immediately.

Grilled Chicken:
¼ cup lemon juice
1 clove garlic, crushed
1 teaspoon salt
1 teaspoon paprika
½ cup olive oil
4 skinless, boneless chicken breast halves (about 4 ounces each)
In a large bowl, whisk together the lemon juice, garlic, salt, and paprika. While whisking, drizzle in the oil until incorporated. Add the chicken, cover, and marinate in the refrigerator for at least 8 hours and up to overnight.

Preheat a stovetop grill pan until hot. Grill the chicken, turning once, until well marked and cooked through, about 15 to 20 minutes. When cool enough to handle, slice very thin and make the sandwiches.

Note: Telera refers to Mexican bread similar to a French roll with a scored and flour-dusted crust. It can be found in Mexican markets, where they're used to make sandwiches called tortas.

Monte Cristo Sandwich

I can remember as a young man in my teens, my father would make up this sandwich. This recipe calls for Gouda cheese; you can use whatever you wish, as long as it is a light creamy cheese. I have tried it with havarti, it worked out great. This recipe is for just one sandwich.

3 slices white bread
mayonnaise, as needed
2 slices Gouda
2 slices turkey
3 large eggs, beaten
1/4 cup milk
2 tablespoons vegetable oil
1 tablespoon unsalted butter

On a flat surface, lay out 2 slices of bread and spread with mayonnaise. Top each slice with the 1 slice of Gouda and 1 slice of turkey each. Put the third slice of bread on top of one stack, and flip the remaining stack on top, cheese-side down, to make a triple-decker sandwich.

Using a knife, cut the crusts off the sandwich (this helps to pinch and seal the ends). Wrap the sandwich tightly with plastic wrap and refrigerate for at least 30 minutes and up to 6 hours. (Wrapping the sandwich in plastic wrap, compacts it, and prevents the egg batter from seeping in.)

Combine the eggs and milk in a bowl. Heat the oil and butter in a skillet over medium-high heat. Unwrap the sandwich and dip it in the egg batter, to coat evenly. Gently place it in the skillet, and fry, turning once, until golden brown and hot, about 5 minutes total.

Cut the Monte Cristo in 1/2, transfer it to a place, and garnish with the strawberry and orange. Spoon some jam over each 1/2 and serve immediately with a darker fruit jam, like blackberry, raspberry, etc.

Pat's Scotch Eggs

I went over my friends Alice and Josie's. Josie's mother was busy in the kitchen and of course, I had to know what she was doing. She explained to me that as a child her mother used to make these scotch eggs for brunch, so I stood over to get a taste, and see what they were all about. I enjoyed them very much and started serving them during holiday brunches.

12 hard boiled eggs
2 lbs. pork sausage
1 cup all purpose flour
2 -3 cups bread crumbs (seasoned)

Take the peeled, towel dried, eggs and roll them in the flour
Coat them with a layer of sausage
Roll in the bread crumbs
Deep fry for 4 minutes

Slice in half
Serve warm

*Note:
I have added chopped onions to the sausage

I have removed the egg yolk and replaced with hollandaise sauce and replaced the yolk

I have completely removed the egg yolk and replaced with finely chopped parsley, onions, pimento and ½ the egg yolks (I like best)

Paula's Quiche Lorraine

One can enjoy this meal anytime of the day.
From breakfast to a late night snack

10" shell – serves 6-8

Shell:
1-10" shell:
1¾ cups all purpose flour
1 teaspoon salt
1¼ sticks chilled butter unsalted
2 tablespoons chilled lard or shortening
1/3 to ½ cup iced water.

Cut lard and butter into flour and salt. Add iced water a very little bit at a time, tossing flour-shortening mixture with a fork. Use as little water as possible to make dough. There should be some dough left over.

Wrap and chill dough for at least 2 hours. Butter the inside of quiche dish. Roll the dough using as little flour as possible. Roll the dough around the rolling pin and unroll over the ring. Press dough into place. To make the sides of the shell strong enough to hold the filling, push dough down the sides of the shell strong enough to hold the filling, push dough down with your fingers all around the ring. Work fast so dough doesn't soften. Roll pin over the top of the ring to remove excess dough. Patch any thin areas with raw dough (will stick if you use a little water). Prick the bottom of the shell with a fork. Cover with plastic wrap and chill 30 minutes so shell will bake evenly. (To freeze, slip the unbaked shell into a plastic bag.) To prevent a soggy bottom, pre-bake the shell. Keep sides and bottom in place by bracing them with buttered foil and dried beans/ macaroni. Bake in 400degrees oven for 6 minutes. Remove the shell from the oven and take out the beans and the foil. With the foil from a light covering over the top crust edge to prevent it from burning. Return the shell to the oven and bake until bottom is very light brown. You are now ready for the filling.

(Continued)

Filling:

6 oz lean bacon unsliced	Cut bacon into small cubes, cook in skillet until not quite crisp. Drain and set aside.
4 eggs and 2 yolks	beat eggs in mixing bowl. Add all remaining ingredients and stir until well blended. Set aside.
3 cups milk (½ cream and ½ milk if preferred) 1tsp salt ¼ white pepper	

Assembly (see page 2)
Assembly:

1 ½ tbsp chopped parsley

1tsp fine herbs (spiced island)

2 clovers garlic, finely chopped

1 large onion	Sautee onions in butter on medium heat until soft but not brown.
2tbsp butter	
6oz Swiss cheese	Grate cheese. Set aside
2tbsp butter	Cut butter into pea-sized dots, place in dish and store in refrigerator to keep solid.

Preheat oven 375degrees

Have ready the pie shell, still in the metal mould.

Distribute the bacon evenly on the bottom of the shell. Follow with onions and next Swiss cheese. Pour the egg mixture into the shell leaving ¼ inch from the top. Distribute the butter pieces on top. Set in upper third of oven and bake for 25 to 30 minutes until quiche has puffed and browned. Unmold and slide quick onto a hot platter. Serve.

Note: For this quiche we used a false bottom flan 10" diameter 2" high with a fluted edge. After it is totally baked, the sides of the flan are removed by placing the flan on a confectionary jar. Once it is stable, you can lower the side and you have an attractive opulent quiche which you will be proud to present to your guests.

The Quickest Grilled Chicken Sandwich Ever

Three weekdays out of five, I am in a rush for dinner. I try to prepare the most tasteful and wholesome meal for my family. This recipe has never gone without the girls asking for seconds or leftovers to take to work or school.

3 chicken breasts halved and sliced in half again
1 large bottle Italian salad dressing (optional)
2 large eggs
1 cup milk
2 cups all purpose flour
1 cup Italian Bread crumbs
1 teaspoon garlic powder
1 tablespoon Paprika
1 teaspoon sugar
dash of salt & pepper
lettuce
tomatoes
red onion
pepper jack cheese
large seeded hamburger buns

Marinate the breasts in a zip lock plastic bag overnight or at least for 2 hours (optional)

Use the eggs and milk as an egg wash.
Combine all other ingredients in a bowl.
Dip the breasts in the egg wash and then toss in the breading.
Drop in a hot deep fryer and fry until golden brown (Chicken should be sliced thin).
Place on a bun with a slice of tomato, lettuce, red onion slice, and pepper jack cheese.

I give the family a choice of barbecue sauce, ranch dressing, plain mayo, or a combination of mayo, hot sauce, and lime juice.

Serve warm with home made French fried potatoes.

<u>Soups</u>

A hot bowl of soup is the way my family always starts off a meal

<u>Dennis' Beef Mushroom Barley Soup</u>

I never thought of enjoying barley soup mixed with mushrooms. Recently, I visited a local New York style deli. Ever so curious, I ordered this soup. I enjoyed it very much. At home I came up with my own rendition of this famous deli soup. I found that using small sliced pieces of beef worked fine, but I prefer to use ox tails (don't let the name scare you), it was superb. The flavor you receive from the bone marrow is excellent. I find the meat a strong flavor, thus enhancing the broth. I sometimes boil potatoes and serve them separately after the soup with a green vegetable. It is now on our regular menu. My daughters Stacy, Stephanie and Ashley quarrel over you get the largest bone!

2 lbs. finely cut -up stewing beef or flank steak (I use Ox tails)
1 medium yellow onion
3 carrots
3 stalks celery
1 medium potato
1 shallot stalk
2 tablespoons beef soup base
4 cloves garlic
2 teaspoons cracked black pepper
2 teaspoons sea salt
¼ cup butter
1 cup raw pearled barley
2 cups sliced fresh button mushrooms

Slice all vegetables ¼ inch and beef in ½ inch cubes, and sauté in butter for 10 minutes with the salt and pepper add 6 quarts of cold water, beef base, and bring to a boil. Hold at a soft boil for 45 minutes.
Add barley and cook until barley is tender (one hour) at a simmer.

Dennis' Sweet Potato & Cheese Soup

I enjoy preparing a typical cream of potato soup. I decided to add a delicate sweet taste by adding a small amount of yam. It brought out a very nice flavor, allowing the soup to have a hint of the sweetness of yams, be careful not to add too many, they can overpower the potato and cheese flavors.

10 russet potatoes clean and cubes
2 large yams cleaned and cubed
1 large onion thin sliced
4 stalks celery thin sliced
3 carrots cubed
3 tablespoons chicken soup base (low salt)
1 lb. sliced bacon
1 lb. package shredded sharp cheese
2 tablespoons cracked black pepper
2 tablespoons seasoning salt
½ teaspoon rosemary
¼ teaspoon crushed red pepper
2 cans evaporated milk
½ gallon regular milk

Fry the bacon until just about crisp.
Add the onions, carrots, and celery and fry for 10 minutes over medium heat.
Add the potatoes and yams, fry until the potatoes begin to lightly brown at the corners
Toss in remaining ingredients except for the cheese.
Transfer to a soup pot and fill ¾ with water and SLOW boil for 1 hour
Add the evaporated milk and regular milk, with a hand potato masher, mash slightly to
  Allow large chunks of potato to remain in the soup.
Add the cheese and simmer until all the cheese melts and blends in.

Dennis' Favorite Cream of Broccoli Soup

In my garden I grew four broccoli plants, once ready for harvest, I realized that there was not enough broccoli to prepare for one meal, since this is one of my families favorite vegetable. I came up with a few ideas that the rest of the family would probably, turn their nose to. I knew my family likes cream of broccoli soup, so it was what I decided to do with my broccoli. I wanted this soup rich and full of flavor, with a hint of a smokey flavor that is where the minced bacon came into the recipe. I served it in a medium soup bowl with a light sprinkle of paprika and a dime size dollop of sour cream in the center, making it as wonderful to the eye as it is for the palette.

4 bunches fresh broccoli
2 large carrots
1 large white onion
1 small scallion
4 strips thick sliced smoked bacon
2 large potatoes
2 medium bay leafs
2 cups strong chicken broth (Made from chicken soup base and hot water)
1 cup shredded smoked cheddar cheese
½ cup Butter
2 tablespoons salt (omit if chicken soup base contains heavy salt)
2 tablespoons black pepper
¼ cup all potato flour or all purpose flour

Peel the stalks of the broccoli and slice thin reserving the tops.
Pinch each small to medium flower of half the broccoli, chopping the other half
Thinly Slice carrots, onions, scallions, and bacon.
Mince celery.
Cut and peel potatoes in small square cubes.

In a soup pot melt butter and sauté all vegetables except for potatoes, and bacon until onions become translucent. Add the bay leaf, salt and pepper. Add potatoes and gently slow simmer in 2 cups chicken broth for 20 minutes allowing the broth to absorb the flavors. Mix well, the cold cream, milk, salt, pepper, and flour. Add to soup, raise heat. And stir slowly. Once at a boil, lower heat to a simmer and simmer ½ hour gently stirring frequently so that the cream mixture does not stick to bottom and burn. Stir in the Cheddar cheese gently stirring not to break apart remaining broccoli flowers. Garnish with a ¼ teaspoon size dollop of butter and a sprinkle of dried parsley and paprika.

Dennis' Tex-Mex Tortilla Soup

I am sure there are hundreds of renditions of this recipe. I for like to prepare it the following way. I find this recipe to have the flavor, but holds back the spiciness. It goes well in the cooler months. This soup can have the tendency to hold a person warm for hours. Enjoy!

1 large onion sliced
3 carrots sliced
3 celery stalks sliced
¼ medium cauliflower segmented
1 green pepper chopped
1 red bell pepper chopped
½ cup corn
1 can stew tomatoes
1½ lbs. ground beef
¼ cup tomato paste
4 tablespoons cumin
4 tablespoons paprika
1 cup raw rice
1 bag regular tortilla chips

Mix the entire recipe except for the Tortilla chips in a large bowl and drain the vegetables well. Place on the stove and cook at a medium Boil for 1 ½ hours. When serving, top with a dollop of sour cream and tortilla chips in the center.

Fish and Rice Soup - (Aljotta)

This is a very light soup. It doesn't sound appetizing, until you have tried it. I enjoy a lighter tasting fish such as cod, red snapper, or baby shrimp. I have seen others use Sea bass, ocean perch and other stronger flavored fish.

2 –3 lbs. Fish fillets
2 Medium Yellow Onions
5 Cloves Garlic
3 Teaspoons Tomato Paste
½ Cup Frozen Peas or Frozen Corn (For Color)
½ Cup White Rice or Ziti Pasta
1 Teaspoon Dried Mint or 4 Sprigs Fresh Mint Leaves
¼ Cup Olive Oil
3 Tablespoons Chicken Soup Base
1 Teaspoon White Pepper
½ Teaspoon Salt

Fry onion and garlic until garlic is browned.
Add the fish (I prefer a light tasting, firm flesh fish) and sauté until tender
Add the fresh herbs, salt and pepper, if chicken base is used, omit the salt
Gently stir in the tomato paste, chicken base and rice or pasta and slowly simmer for 15 minutes, gently stirring
Fill pot with water and slow boil until rice is cooked but still slightly firm

Serve with a few this slices of lemon, and a sprig of mint floating in the center.

Manuel's Maltese Style Stuffed Chicken - (Tigiega Bil-Haxu)

The American community is used to a bread stuffing. I laughed the first I was introduced to this stuffing. I always had a meat stuffing served in our holiday turkey or chicken. I must admit, I like the bread stuffing's better, but I still prepare this stuffing for my Maltese relatives, especially my Mother. Maltese cuisine calls for placing a stuffed chicken in a basic vegetable soup instead of baking it. But will stuff a turkey and roast accordingly.

For chicken:
1 large stewing chicken
1 ½ lb. ground round
1 large onion chopped
4 clove garlic chopped
½ cup fresh parsley or ¼ cup dried
½ cup bread crumbs
2 large eggs

For soup:
3 carrots peeled and sliced
3 stalks celery sliced
1 large onion sliced
1 teaspoon Italian seasonings
2 tablespoons chicken soup base

Mix all stuffing ingredients and stuff in the cavity of the chicken.
In a soup pot place all the ingredients including the chicken, fill with water and simmer until the chicken is fully cooked. I like to boil a few potatoes in the soup and lift them out just before serving the soup. The once the chicken is served, place the potatoes around the chicken. You can also once the chicken and potatoes have been removed, add some type of pasta to the soup, allowing the chicken to breathe and settle.

Manuel's (Dad's) Kawlotta

I can remember enjoying this soup as far as I can go back. Minestra is a very traditional winter harvest soup. It is full of flavor and warmth on chilly days. I, enjoy it year round. I especially like it with smoked pork hocks, I boil a few potatoes whole removing them when fully cooked. After enjoying the soup, I place the pork hocks in a dish with the boiled potatoes and a few sliced raw tomatoes drizzled with olive oil. Don't let the pumpkin scare you, it gives this soup "sweet" taste, also gives the soup a wonderful thickness. Experiment! This soup originally was made from whatever was in you refrigerator. It doesn't necessarily call for all the ingredients, omit some and add others. Whatever you like, but remember, the pumpkin is what gives it the distinctive flavor.

*Note Kawlotta has meat in it but Minestra is vegetarian and can be made the same way omitting the meat.

1 large onion sliced
3 carrots sliced into ¼ inch segments
4 celery stalks sliced into ¼ inch segments
1 medium cauliflower pulled into small sections
1 medium cabbage sliced ¼ inch thick
2 cups chopped squash any type as long as it is orange in color (I like pumpkin)
1 cup mixed beans (Lima, Kidney, Navy) any kind will do
½ cup dried green and or yellow peas
1 cup small soup pasta (small elbow works great)
1/8 cup chicken soup base
3 ham hocks or any other smoked meat (Less fatty meats are better)
2 Tablespoons Italian seasonings
2 tablespoons sea salt
1 tablespoon garlic powder
½ cup grated Parmesan cheese

In a large soup pot add everything, except the pasta and cheese, bring to a boil. Boil gently for 2 ½ hours.
Add Pasta and Cheese and boil until the meat is very tender.
Serve with hard crust bread and top with more Parmesan cheese.

Robin's French Onion Soup

My wife Robin enjoys this as often as she possibly can. If the establishment has this on the menu, she is sure to order it. I tweaked it my way be adding even amounts of beef and chicken stock, which adds a more distinctive flavor. I adapted this technique from a restaurant-bar downtown Detroit called the Blues Kitchen Saloon.

2 tablespoons butter
3 large white onions thin sliced and separated
½ teaspoon bay leaves
½ quart chicken stock
½ quart beef stock
6 slices French bread, toasted
3 cups Gruyere Cheese, grated
½ cup sherry wine
Salt and pepper

Heat oil in skillet and add onions, cook and toss until clear.
Add Thyme and bay leaves in butter. Cook until light brown.
Add stocks and simmer 20 minutes and add salt and pepper to taste.
Pour into bowls, add croutons and top with cheese, run under hot broiler until brown.

Sliders

Sliders are in this part of the country, are small hamburgers. In the south, they are dumplings. My wife Robin makes this a few times per year. When this takes place, the family, devours this dish until it is all gone.

6 chicken wings
2 or 3 chicken cubes
Dash salt
Parsley flakes
Flour

Put above in a medium sized pot, add water and simmer for 1 ½ hours.

Noodles:
Take out ½ cup of the broth, put into freezer for 10 minutes. Put one cup of flour into a bowl. Mix a little bit of broth at a time with the flour. Roll it out thinly and cut into squares.
Bring the pot of broth up to a boil again, make sure it is boiling. Add the squares and cook them for 10-15 minutes.
This is a dish which the Gemus family used to really enjoy when they were growing up (that is Lionel's generation) and it is good to see it brought back. To popularity again.

Sweet Chili

This chili will go over well with young children and those who are not very keen on spicy foods. It is a sweet yet flavorful chili that goes well with hot dogs or hamburgers for a quick fall afternoon meal.

2 cans kidney beans
5 cans stewed tomatoes
1½ lbs. lean ground beef
1 medium chopped onion
3 whole clove stems
2 bay leaves
½ teaspoon chili powder
2 tablespoons sugar
½ teaspoon garlic powder

Fry the ground beef in a few drops of vegetable oil.
Add the chopped onion, garlic, salt, and pepper.
In a large pot add the remaining ingredients and simmer for 1 hour, stirring occasionally.

Zapata Tuscana

I met Dave Brown at a roofing plant in Byron Center Michigan. We began to chat about cooking; this is one of his prized recipes he came up with. I tried it and it was fabulous

¼ lb bacon
¾ lb hot Italian sausage
½ cup diced onion
2 cloves crushed minced garlic
1 quart water
2 table spoon chicken soup base
2 cups chopped kale
3 regular potato's peeled and sliced ¼ inch thick
½ cup heavy whipping cream

Bake sausage in 350 degree oven till done
Place bacon in large sauce pan cook bacon till crisp then remove
Sweat onions in the bacon grease when almost translucent
Add garlic give it a chance before you
Add water soup-base and potatoes to the pot
When potatoes are all most tender add whipping cream
Then add Bacon, Sausage, and Kale heat and sever
I like to add little crushed red peppers to my bowl, little extra heat

Salads

Always start off your meal with some type of salad. In European countries, the salad is eaten last to cleanse the pallet.

Crunchy Oriental Salad with Peanut Sauce

This recipe is full of color, and flavor. This salad would be the center of attention On anyone's table. A kitchen mandolin would be very helpful.

1 head thinly sliced romaine lettuce
1 head thinly sliced white cabbage
2 thinly sliced carrots
1 thinly sliced medium red onions
2 thinly sliced green onions
¼ cup chopped fresh cilantro
1 package of wonton skins sliced in strips. (save some for the garnish)
½ cup natural smooth peanut butter
¼ cup seasoned rice vinegar
1 tablespoon warm water
½ teaspoon red pepper flakes
3 teaspoon toasted sesame oil
2 teaspoons soy sauce
1 teaspoon white sugar

Combine lettuce, cabbage, carrots, ½ the crunchy noodles, and onions
  in a large mixing bowl.
Whisk together the peanut butter, vinegar, pepper flakes, sesame oil, soy
  sauce, and sugar (If the dressing is still too thick, add a little water until
  the preferred consistence)
Toss the salad mixture with the dressing and place on a large decorative
  platter, forming a mountain shape and top with the remaining noodles
  and cilantro

Dennis' Oriental Teriyaki Mandarin Chicken Over fresh Salad Greens

I visited many establishments with this particular meal on their menus. I realized
it being so popular and knew that I must try my own rendition of this recipe. After
many summer nights experimenting around the dinner table, my family decided

that this combination tastes best. Try it with a fresh smoothie beverage and you
think you are in heaven.

3 chicken breasts
2 medium carrots
½ medium onion
1 small scallion
6 button mushrooms
1 bunch green onions (stalks and all)
6 Lee-Chee nuts (meat only) optional
1 small red plum
¼ cup raisins (optional)
1 cup sesame oil
¼ cup vegetable oil
¼ cup seasoned rice vinegar
4 tablespoons wine vinegar
4 tablespoons soy sauce
2 tablespoons white sugar
2 teaspoons garlic powder
2 teaspoons onion powder
1 tablespoons Kosher salt
1 tablespoon white pepper
2-3 dashes of hot sauce (Tabasco)
2 small cans Mandarin orange segments (juice and all)
1 bunch romaine lettuce
1 bunch spinach
1 small Iceberg lettuce

NIGHT BEFORE:
Marinate sliced raw chicken breasts in teriyaki marinate for 1 hour.
Sauté over medium heat while constantly draining out all the liquid from the frying
pan as the chicken sweats. After almost, if not all, the moisture is drained, add ¼
cup good grade vegetable oil and sauté until chicken is done to just medium.
Put in an airtight container and chill overnight in the refrigerator.
I use a commercial teriyaki marinate. You can make your own by mixing 2 part
of soy sauce, 1 part Brown Sugar, 1 Part Honey and ½ Part Crushed Ginger.

(Continued)

Day of serving:

In a metal bowl, Sliver the following:

chilled chicken breasts prepared the day before
2 medium carrots
½ medium onion
1 small scallion
6 button mushrooms
1 bunch green onions (stalks and all)
6 Lee-Chee nuts (meat only) optional
1 small red plum
¼ cup raisins (optional)

Soak in 1 cup of the following, reserving the remaining for serving as the Dressing.

1 cup sesame oil
¼ cup Vegetable oil
¼ cup seasoned rice vinegar
4 tablespoons wine vinegar
4 tablespoons soy sauce
2 tablespoons white sugar
2 teaspoons garlic powder
2 teaspoons onion powder
1 tablespoons kosher salt
1 tablespoon white pepper
1 dash hot sauce (Tabasco)
2 small cans mandarin orange segments (Juice and all)

In an airtight container, gently flip all ingredients not to tear the orange segments and soak for at least, ½ hour turning at least every 10 minutes.

hand tear the following:
1 bunch romaine lettuce
1 small iceberg lettuce
1 small bunch chard
1 small bunch spinach

Any other combinations of salad greens can be used. Whatever your preference is.
Place a bed of salad greens mixture on a salad bowl; add the chicken/veggie combination, top with chopped walnuts and Chinese canned noodles.

Spinach, Mushroom and Bacon Salad
My family has always liked spinach (except for Robin). This is a fresh salad that can be enjoyed as a meal. Serve it with fresh garlic bread and a bowl of soup for a healthy meal.

1 lb. spinach, coarse stems discarded and leaves washed well and
spun dried (about 6 cups)
3 slices of bacon, cooked until crisp, drained and crumbled.
5 mushrooms, sliced thin
2 scallions, minced
¼ spinach salad dressing

Toss all ingredients well, drizzle with salad dressing and re-toss.

Spinach Salad Dressing:

¼ cup fresh lemon juice
1 large raw egg yolk (if you have a problem with raw
egg yolks substitute 1 tbsp of mayonnaise)
¾ teaspoon salt
½ teaspoon dry mustard
¼ teaspoon freshly ground black pepper
¼ teaspoon sugar
1 very small garlic clove, chopped
1 cup olive oil

In a food processor blend all ingredients except oil until smooth. With motor
running add oil in a stream, blending until emulsified. Transfer dressing to a jar
and keep chilled, covered, until serving, makes about 1 ¼ cups.

Serves 4

Mediterranean Potato Salad

I like to use this recipe in the latter part of the summer when everyone is tired of
the same old mayonnaise based potato salads. Remember it does best when
you can allow the dish to stand for at least an hour before serving.

2 lbs. small new or red skinned potatoes (unpeeled), boiled fork-tender
½ cup dry wine (can be substituted with chicken broth)
1 medium red onion
½ cup pitted ripe black olives sliced
4 green onions, finely chopped
½ cup sun dried tomatoes in oil, drained and chopped
½ cup bottled balsamic or re wine vinaigrette
½ cup fresh flat leaf parsley, chopped

Take potatoes and if preferred, may be peeled (I leave the peel on) and cut in quarters.
In a large bowl, toss all ingredients, except parsley and let stand for an hour at room temperature.
Toss in parsley just before serving.

One Pot Meals

This section was designed for those who are always in a hurry. Most of these meals can prepared with a crock-pot.

Cabbage Rolls - Lionel Gemus

Cabbage is my favorite Polish entrée. I like to invite friends over for what I call a Polish feast. I prepare cabbage rolls, pierogi, and kielbasa with mashed potatoes and sauce used to bake the cabbage in or sour kraut. Scrumptious!

1/3 cup raw rice
2 cups milk
1 lb. ground meat (I like to use beef & pork)
1 teaspoon seasoned salt
1 teaspoon Worchester sauce
5 drops Tabasco
2 medium eggs
½ teaspoon salt
1 medium onion
¼ teaspoon celery salt
1 tablespoon Romano cheese

12 cabbage leaves, soaked in boiling water until pliable.

Cook rice in 1 cup milk over double boiler. Cool. Add rest of mild and remaining ingredients (better be careful with that salt—this is an old recipe and we don't use as much salt as we used to). Place 1 ½ of the recipe in a cabbage leaf, roll up as with an envelope. Brown slowly in bacon fat. Pour off excess grease.

Mix:
1 cup boiling water
1 bouillon cube
2 tablespoons brown sugar
Small can mushroom pieces of juice.

Pour over rolls, cover simmer 1 hr, basting and turning occasionally.
Remove rolls, thicken liquid with 1 tbsp flour, stir in ½ tsp vinegar and serve sauce with rolls.

Dennis' Cabbage Rolls
There are many different recipes for cabbage rolls. I prefer this one. It has a nice light flavor, adding the slivered bacon gives it a nice little extra taste. I like to invite friends over for what I call a Polish feast. I prepare cabbage rolls, pierogi,

and kielbasa with mashed potatoes and sauce used to bake the cabbage in or sour kraut. Scrumptious!

1/3 cup raw rice (I use Jasmine)
1 lb. ground meat (I like to use beef & pork)
1 teaspoon seasoned salt
5 drops Tabasco
2 medium eggs
½ teaspoon salt
1 medium onion
¼ teaspoon celery salt
1 tablespoon Romano cheese
4 strips cooked slivered bacon
2 teaspoons fresh parsley
4-6 medium potatoes peeled and left whole

12 cabbage leaves, soaked in boiling water until pliable. Or freeze overnight then allow to thaw naturally.

Par boil rice, and cool. Add rest of mild and remaining ingredients Place 1 ½ of the recipe in a cabbage leaf, roll up as with an envelope. Brown slowly in vegetable oil. Pour off excess grease.

Mix:
2 cans Campbell's tomato soup
1 cup boiling water
1 bouillon cube
1 cup frozen peas
Small can mushroom pieces of juice.

Pour cold sauce over rolls, cover and place in the oven at 350 degrees for 1 hour, uncover and raise the temperature to 500 degrees, bake for an additional 10 minutes or until the tips of the cabbage turn brown.
Boil potatoes until tender.
Serve the cabbage rolls with whole boiled potatoes. Pour the sauce over the top of the potatoes and cabbage rolls, and serve with a simple green salad and crusty bread.

Dennis' Stuffed Flank Steak Soup

This recipe is a complete meal. It has the soup, and after the meat and vegetables. Back in Malta, a family did not have the convenience of a modern stove. So the cook of the house would prepare everything in one pot, making it less complicated, and taking up less room in the small kitchen. My father used to make this occasionally, he used all the freshest ingredients, beginning in the morning and serving it late in the afternoon. Potatoes are a common vegetable to serve with this meat, keeping them whole, and allowing them to absorb the soups flavor.

Before we start, when purchasing a flank steak, ask the butcher to cut a "pocket" into it. Once this is finished, it will resemble a Kangaroo pouch where you will add the stuffing.

1-2 to 3 lb. flank steak

FOR STUFFING:
½ lb ground beef
½ lb. ground lean pork
1 large chopped onion
4 cloves chopped garlic
½ cup grated Parmesan cheese
½ cup chopped fresh parsley
½ cup seasoned Italian crumbs
2 large eggs
1 teaspoon rosemary
1 teaspoon basil

FOR SOUP:
4 –6 (depending how many served, 1 per person) medium potatoes left whole
2 large yellow onions sliced
3 carrots peeled and cleaned cut into 1 inch wedges
4 stalks celery cut into 1 inch wedges
1 can stewed tomatoes
2 tablespoons beef soup base
1 tablespoon white pepper
1 teaspoon Italian spices
½ teaspoon Sugar

Place entire ingredients into a large soup pot and fill with 5 quarts water. Place the stuffed flank steak into the pot and boil. Boil at a medium boil for 1 hour bringing down the heat and slowly boiling the soup combination for an additional 2 hours. Test the flank steak, once done, pull it out and place in a large serving plate along with the potatoes. Serve the soup first, then one time to slightly cool and breathe, slice the flank steak in 1 inch thick slices and place in the center of the servings plate with the potatoes around the outside of the meat. Best served with a green vegetable and a loaf of a hard crust Italian style loaf of bread.

Lamb Stew

Lamb stew is a staple meal for the Irish. The meat and vegetable combination make this a one pot meal that will fulfill even the hungriest member at you dinner table.

1/4 cup vegetable oil

Flour, for dredging

21/2 pounds lamb shoulder, cut into 2-inch cubes, or purchase precut lamb stew meat

4 teaspoons kosher salt

Freshly ground black pepper

2 tablespoons unsalted butter

2 medium onions, cut into sixths

5 cloves garlic, minced

1 tablespoon tomato paste

10 cups cold water, or low-sodium chicken broth

6 sprigs parsley

6 sprigs fresh thyme

2 bay leaves

11/4 pounds medium red potatoes, quartered

4 medium carrots, cut into 1-inch pieces

2 celery stalks, cut into 1-inch pieces

7 canned whole, peeled tomatoes, lightly crushed

1 tablespoon red wine vinegar

Heat a large Dutch oven with a tight-fitting lid over medium-high heat. Pour in enough oil to fill the pan about 1/4-inch deep. Spread flour out on a plate or piece of waxed paper. Season half the lamb with 1 teaspoon of the salt and some pepper. Dredge in the flour and shake off the excess. Cook, uncovered, stirring only occasionally, until well browned, about 8 minutes. Using a slotted spoon, transfer the lamb to a plate. Repeat with the remaining lamb. Discard the oil and wipe out the pan. Preheat the oven to 275 degrees F. Return the pot to the stove and melt the butter over medium-high heat. Add the onion and cook, stirring, until lightly browned, about 5 minutes. Stir in the garlic and tomato paste and cook until fragrant, about 2 minutes. Return the lamb to the pot and add the water or broth, and bring to a simmer. Using a piece of kitchen twine, tie together the parsley, thyme, and bay leaves and add the bundle to the pot. Stir in the remaining 2 teaspoons salt and pepper. Cover and transfer to the oven. Stew the meat until tender, about 1 1/2 hours. Remove the Dutch oven from the oven. Skim the fat from the cooking liquid with a ladle. Add the potatoes, carrots, celery, and the tomatoes, and bring to a simmer. Cook the stew, uncovered, on top of the stove until the liquid has thickened and the vegetables are tender, about 1 hour. Remove and discard the herb bundle. Stir in the vinegar. Divide among bowls and serve immediately.

Cajun Jambalaya – Lionel Gemus

Who can refuse a steaming dish of Jambalaya? This is definitely one of my favorite recipes I have collected from my friend Mike's father. I tried it, and realized I made one mistake. I made it when the house filled up with unexpected guests, next time I have to double the amount called for.

1lb. smoked sausage
½ lb. ham
4 oz. butter
4 tablespoons flour
3 medium onions, chopped
4 cloves of garlic, chopped
6 green onions, chopped
1 cup celery, chopped
1 cup green pepper, chopped
2 oz. tomato paste
1 bay leaf
½ teaspoon thyme
1/8 teaspoon cumin
1/8 teaspoon cloves
1/8 teaspoon all spice
1/8 teaspoon cayenne pepper
¼ teaspoon black pepper
2 cups rice, raw
¼ cup parsley chopped
3 cupsbeef stock
1 cup cooked chicken, chopped

Cut ham and sausage into pieces. Sautee sausage and ham in butter in a large pot. Remove and set aside.
Add flour to pot and cook 5 minutes. Add onions, garlic, green onions, celery, and green pepper. Add tomatoes and tomato paste. Add bay leaf, thyme, cumin, cloves, allspice, cayenne and black pepper. Stir in raw rice. Add parsley. Pour in the beef broth. Add salt (if necessary) to taste. Return sausage and ham a long with the chicken to the mixture.
Bring to a boil. Lower heat to simmer. Cover and cook for about 20 minutes until the liquid is absorbed.

Loraine's Black Skillet Beef with Greens and Red Potatoes
Now this one dish meal is just out of this world. The thin strips of meat and vegetables, make it an unusual stew. Serve it on a cold winter day, the meat,

potatoes and veggies will warm the most coldest tummies. It is a rendition of beef stew, but full of southern soul.

2 lbs. beef top round
3 teaspoons Hot 'N Spicy seasoning
12 red skinned potatoes, halved
5 cup finely chopped onions
4 cups beef broth
5 large cloves garlic, minced
4 large carrots, cut into very thin 2 ½ inch strips
2 bunches (1/2 lb. each) mustard green, kale or turnip greens, stems removed
  Coarsely torn
Olive oil

Partially freeze beef.
Slice the beef as thin as possible across the grain into long strips 1/8 inch thick.
Thoroughly coat the strips with the Hot 'N Spice seasonings.
Coat a heavy skillet with olive oil (cast iron Dutch oven works best).
Preheat over high heat, just before oil begins to smoke, add the beef.
Cook for five minutes, it is important to rapidly stir the meat so that it does not incur any burn marks.
Add entire ingredients except for the carrots and simmer over medium heat for 30 minutes.
Stir in the carrots and keep simmering for an additional 15 minutes.
Serve in a soup bowl with plenty of broth, with crusty bread for dunking.

Manuel's Chicken Stew

Growing up as in a Maltese household, Stew was a meal we ate often. In Malta, stewing tough cuts of meat during the war was a way to allow the family to consume a wholesome meal. Combining the vegetables and meats, placing them in a large pot made from either clay or metal. Mom would walk down to the baker where his wood burning stove was hot from baking bread all morning. She would give him a few coins to allow him to place dinner into his oven, where she returned after her daily chores.

Either beef, meatballs, pork, just about any cut of meat may be used. It is your choice, my father put together the best stews I ever tasted. Just full of homemade flavor, nothing extravagant, they were always hearty and appetizing. We usually enjoyed this meal with a loaf of hard crust bread, sometimes over a bed of white rice.

1 chicken cut into 8 pieces washed and drained
3 large Idaho potatoes in 2-inch cubes
3 large carrots sliced every ½ inch
2 medium onions (halved)
3 stalks celery, cut into ¼ inch sections
4 cloves garlic chopped
½ cup extra virgin olive oil
½ cup semi-sweet white wine
3 cups chicken stock or chicken soup base
2 medium Bay leafs
1 teaspoon sea salt
1 teaspoon white pepper
1 teaspoon Italian spices
¼ cup raisins (optional)
flour, arrowroot, or corn starch

Wash and pat dry chicken and fry in half the amount of olive oil
At medium heat until brown throughout.
Add vegetables and spices, add remaining oil reduce the heat and
Simmer until carrots begin to become tender but still firm.
Add the chicken stock /base and simmer at low heat until the carrots,
and potatoes are tender.
Mix enough thickener (start off with 2 tablespoons) with ½ cup cold
Water, and add to the stew.
Toss in raisins and wine, simmer an additional 20 minutes.
May be served with rice or risotto.

Manuel's (Dad's) Hearty Beef Stew

This dish calls for beef. Nothing says it must be beef, I have used lean pork. Whatever you and your family prefer. The beef in this recipe calls for cubed stew beef, my father, Nana (grandmother), and aunt used Ox tails or beef short ribs, making this dish to die for. Nothing in this book demands every recipe followed exactly, experiment as I did. My family loves Maltese cooking, but to accommodate everyone, I use an American flair.

3 lbs. cubed stewing beef
2 large yellow onions quartered
3 large carrots peeled and sliced in 2 inch segments
1 whole garlic bulb peeled and sliced
4 medium potatoes quartered
½ cup frozen green peas
2 teaspoons kosher salt
2 teaspoons Pepper
2 large dried Bay leafs
3 teaspoons beef soup base
¼ teaspoon rosemary
½ teaspoon dried basil
3 cups cold water
4 tablespoons flour or corn starch
½ cup red wine (optional)
½ cup olive oil
¼ cup dried raisins (optional)

Fry the onions, garlic, potatoes, and carrots in the olive oil for 15 minutes.
Add the remaining ingredients except for the, flour or cornstarch, wine, raisins, and peas and simmer for 1 ½ hours.
Pull out the basil leaves
Add the peas, and raisins, in a small cup or bowl, add the thickening agent and a small amount of water. Once the peas thaw out in the stew, pour in the thickening agent, gently stir and very slow simmer for an additional ½ hour. This dish may be served over white rice, and served with Maltese crusty breads.

Stuffed Green Zucchini in Vegetable Soup

This is a great one pot meal. Everything goes into a stock pot, the meat, the vegetables, and to top it off, the soup is included. can't do much more for a complete meal.

4 large zucchini (Thick enough so that a teaspoon can fit in the center)

STUFFING:
1 lb. lean ground beef
1 medium to large onion
5 cloves of garlic
½ cup dried parsley or
1 cup fresh parsley (better, but not always available)
½ cup seasoned Italian bread crumbs
¼ cup finely grated Romano cheese
1/8 teaspoon of each salt and white pepper

SOUP:
4 medium potatoes (halved)
½ the zucchini meat honed out
2 large carrots sliced in ½ inch segments
1 medium onion sliced
½ cup sliced celery sliced in ½ inch segments
2 –3 tablespoons tomato paste
½ teaspoon of each salt and white pepper
¼ cup chicken base (unsalted preferred) if unavailable then use
¼ cup regular chicken or beef soup base and omit the salt in the broth only
1 cup rice or preferred soup pasta (amount is your decision).

Cut the stem and hone out zucchini with a teaspoon just to the bottom,
But, not going completely through, setting the honed out meat of the
Vegetable to the side, Store in a bowl of iced water, and set aside.
in a bowl, mix ground beef, minced onion and garlic, seasoned breadcrumbs, parsley, grated Romano cheese salt and pepper.
Carefully fill the stuffing into the hollow dried zucchini cavity, and place
in the bottom of a soup pot.
Add sliced onion, ½ the small cubed meat of the zucchini, carrots, celery, zucchini meat, and tomato paste and salt and pepper to taste. Add either chicken or beef soup base and fill with cold water enough so that the liquids edge is 1 inch from the top of your soup pot.
Set on a high flame until liquid begins to boil partially cover, and simmer for 1 hour.

(Continued)

Add potatoes cut in half, rice or any pasta to your preference, and simmer until the potatoes are tender.

Once potatoes are tender, carefully lift the potatoes and zucchini from the soup pot, if necessary, add more water and bring back to a simmer, otherwise, serve soup. Once soup is consumed, serve the zucchini and potatoes together, drizzling a very small amount of olive oil over the potatoes and zucchini.

Serve with a green vegetable such as steamed spinach.

Pasta with Kielbasa, Tomatoes and Bell peppers

I have heard of this recipe for a number of years. I finally decided to give it a shot. Simply a great alternative way to prepare kielbasa.

Non-stick oven-proof skillet
1lb. Kielbasa, skinned, cut in ½ to 1" pieces
3 tablespoons vegetable oil
2 large onion, finely chopped
1 large tomatoes, plunged into boiling water, skinned, seeds removed, and diced
1 bell pepper, red or green, finely chopped
8oz. pasta, bow ties or similar
1 ½ cup dry red or white wine
Parmesan cheese

Pre-set oven 350 degrees
Cook pasta in boiling water until el dente, cool and set aside in cold water

In skillet sauté onion in oil, at medium heat until soft.
Add kielbasa and cook 4 minutes.
Add tomatoes, pepper, stirring all the while.
Add pasta and continue cooking over low heat for 8 minutes.
Add wine, salt, and pepper to taste.
Stir thoroughly.
Sprinkle with parmesan cheese.
Place skillet in oven for 30 minutes.
Serve hot.

Robins Sheppard's Pie

Whenever my wife Robin has time to spare, she usually prepares a great meal. One of my favorites is her shepherd's pie. This is what was considered a peasant food. Cheap and fast. I disagree, she takes the time and effort to make this a pleasant meal for the entire family.

2 lbs. ground sirloin
1 medium onion
2 cloves crushed garlic
1 small bag frozen mixed vegetables
Pinch rosemary
1 can brown gravy
Mashed potatoes (fresh)

Brown the ground beef with the onions and garlic.
Add the remaining ingredients except for the mashed potatoes
In a baking dish, place the meat mixture on the bottom.
Top with the mashed potatoes, brush a small amount of butter .
(May be topped off with shredded sharp cheese for the last 5 minutes of baking)
Bake at 350 degrees for 45 minutes

Side Dishes

Vegetables, Legumes, Beans and Rice

Serving the side dish is as important as the main entrée. Always consider what goes best with the meat you are providing.

Aunt Guza's Special Potatoes

These are the most simple and pleasing potatoes. It is a flavorful side dish with the taste of garlic and butter. Don't hesitate on experimenting with this recipe. It is simple enough to add more of your own ingredients to satisfy your taste. This is an excellent side dish with grilled steak. At times, I have placed a small ladle of brown gravy over the steak and potatoes making it suburb.

6 – 8 russet potatoes
2 large thin sliced onions
1 bulb chopped garlic
1 teaspoon cumin
1 teaspoon white pepper
2 tablespoons sea salt
3 tablespoons dried parsley or ¼ cup fresh
¼ cup olive oil

Par boil potatoes until tender, and rinse under ice cold water
In olive oil, sauté onions and garlic
Cube potatoes two-inch squares and add to frying pan
Add spices and fry potatoes until golden brown on all four sides
Be careful not to crumble potatoes, do this over medium heat.

Dennis' Fried Cabbage with Eggs

A side dish that is too easy to taste this good. My father would serve this with ea fried steak. My daughters expect this to be served at least twice a month.

1 extra large cabbage (sliced)
4 large eggs
½ cup Parmesan cheese
½ cup chicken stock
2 tablespoons garlic powder
1 teaspoon sugar
   olive oil
   salt and pepper to taste

Sweat the cabbage in the chicken stock just before all the liquid evaporates
In a large pan with the hot olive oil place the cabbage being very careful not to splatter the oil. Sauté` over medium heat until the cabbage begins to brown. Add the dry ingredients and toss mixing well. Beat the eggs and fold in until the eggs are full cooked. Serve piping hot.

Dennis' Best Fried Cabbage Ever

Growing up in Corktown as a young man never had any cabbage on our dinner table. Raised predominantly Maltese, my family rarely served any other ethnic cuisine. I started to experiment with other flavors from around the globe, and I once visited a small tea room in Corktown that served a sautéed cabbage side. It was great. I took this recipe to another level adding a few more flavors that compliment the vegetable. I feel this is one everyone will enjoy.

1 large cabbage quartered and thin sliced
2 medium onions sliced
6 cloves minced garlic
2 medium carrots peeled and minced
6 strips crispy bacon slivered
½ cup fresh chopped parsley or ¼ cup dried parsley
¼ cup grated parmesan cheese
1 tablespoon sea salt
1 teaspoon black pepper
Olive oil

In a large skillet, sauté the garlic and carrots over low-medium heat until tender.
Add entire ingredients except for cheese and sauté for 25 minutes.
Top with the cheese and sauté for an additional 10 minutes.

Dennis' Black-Eyed Peas

It is said the first meal of the New Year for good luck should be black eyed peas. I will admit, that I never thought I would enjoy these beans. I tried it a few years ago and it was not on my favorite's list. Until a friend Paula made it for me to welcome in the New Year. I changed the meat used to season. Paula uses salt pork which is very good as in her rendition of this recipe in this section, but I find that using smoked turkey legs give it a different smoky flavor. It is up to your taste buds, both are great. This is a very easy side dish; it may even be served as a light meal with a hunk of warm corn bread.

2 lbs. dried black-eyed peas
3 small smoked turkey legs
1 large finely chopped yellow onion
4 minced garlic cloves
2 teaspoons salt
1 tablespoon black pepper
6 cups water

Put it all together in a large pot and simmer until the beans are tender.

Dennis' Black Beans and Rice – Costa Rican Style

After enjoying this meal, you wonder why we must eat meat everyday. A few years back, I decided to become a vegetarian; it lasted for two years until it became too difficult to prepare two meals, one for my family, and one for myself.

2 onions, medium size, chopped
4 cloves garlic, crushed
3 stalks celery, chopped
1-6 oz. can tomato paste
3-15 oz. cans black beans, drained
2 cups brown rice cooked in 4 cups water
2 Bay leaves
1 teaspoon oregano, dried
1 teaspoon cilantro, dried
   hot red pepper sauce (to taste)

Place 4 cups of water in a pot with cover set on stovetop and heat until boiling.
Add 2 cups raw brown long grain rice and stir.
When water begins to boil again, stir, and reduce heat to simmer, don't stir again. The rice should be done in about 20-30 minutes.
While rice is cooking, wash and peel onions and chop into small pieces.
Wash and chop celery stalks.
Sautee the onions, garlic cloves, and add to baking dish, now toss in the hot sauce, bay leaves, oregano and cilantro and celery until soft.
When the vegetables are cooked, add drained black beans and tomato paste.
Wash out the tomato paste can with some water, add this water to the dish, and stir frequently.
When Rice is cooked, add to other ingredients together in a baking dish and stir well.
Heat in a 350 degree oven for 20 minutes or until hot. Add additional Hot Sauce to taste.
Remove bay leaves before serving.
Serve as is, or Spoon Black Beans and Rice onto warmed tortillas.

Dennis Crock Pot Beans

Very easy without any fuss at all. Any type of bean may be used, I like pinto and great northern but that is my preference.

Soak the beans in water and a little salt for 4 hours before using.

2 lbs. dried beans
1 large fine chopped onion
6 cloves garlic minced
1 tablespoons pepper
2 teaspoons season salt
1 teaspoon crushed celery seed
2 lbs. smoked meat (turkey, neck bones, salt pork, etc.)
6 cups water

Place all in a crock pot.
Place on high walk away for 10 hours.
Serve with warm corn bread.

.

Paula's Black-Eyed Peas

It is said that the first meal of the New Year is a bowl of black eyed peas. I will admit, that I never thought I would enjoy these beans. I tried it a few years back and it was not on my favorite's list. Until a friend Paula made it for me to welcome in the New Year. This is a very easy side dish; it may even be served as a light meal with a hunk of warm corn bread.

2 lbs. dried black-eyed peas
½ lb. chunked salt pork
1 large finely chopped yellow onion
4 minced garlic cloves
2 teaspoons salt
1 tablespoon black pepper
6 cups water

Put it all together in a large pot and simmer until the beans are tender

Dennis' Deluxe Rice

I prepare this recipe as a main dish (or snack). I have made it for dinner, but have not been able to serve it, my girls would eat it before I can serve it with a main dish!

3 cups Jasmine rice
1 can canned corned beef
½ cup vegetable oil
1 medium onion thin sliced
1 teaspoon garlic powder
1 teaspoon cracked black pepper
1 tablespoons seasoning salt
1 – 2 envelope(s) sasoon
  (Sasoon is a seasoning that comes in individual envelopes in a box. Can be
    that purchased in most Latin grocery mkt.)
1 ½ cups water or chicken broth

Combine all except for the water in a large pot and mix well until the corned beef is in very small crumbs.
Add water and place on high heat until a rapid boil.
Bring down to a slow simmering boil and boil until the liquid disappears

DO NOT STIR EXCEPT ONE TIME TO MIX EVERYTHING WHEN THE LIQUID STARTS TO BOIL.

Dennis' Dirty Rice

As a side or as the main course, this recipe can be used for both. I enjoy this dish very much with warm corn bread and a cold beer.

3 ¾ cups chicken steamed and cubed
2 cups smoked sausage cubed
1½ cups uncooked rice
½ tsp cayenne pepper
¼ cup butter
½ cup coarsely ground chicken livers
½ cup coarsely ground chicken gizzards
½ cup coarsely ground raw pork (4oz)
¾ cup chopped onions
½ cup chopped celery
½ cup chopped green pepper
½ cup chopped green onion tops
2 tablespoons minced garlic

Bring 2 ¼ cups chicken stock to a boil in a 4 quart saucepan.
Add the chicken, cook and remove, allow to cool then cube into 1 inch cubes.
Add the rice to the chicken stock and cook until rice has absorbed all the chicken stock, 20-25 minutes over low heat. When complete, the rice should be somewhat dry and not completely cooked.
Meanwhile, melt the butter in another 4 quart saucepan and Sautee the chicken livers, gizzards and pork until brown.
All other ingredients including the cubed chicken, except the stock and rice, cook for 20 minutes on medium heat.
Add the stock, boil on medium high for 15 minutes. Stir in 4 cups cooked rice and cook until all stock is absorbed. Bake in oven for 10-15 minutes at 350 degrees.
Yield: 6-8 servings.

Dennis' Grilled Garden Vegetables Medley

This is a very simple recipe that is full of color as well as flavor. I usually serve this when grilling outdoors among friends and family, where I could brag of the time and effort it took to prepare (little did they know). I have even tried placing the vegetables on top of a bed of rice seasoned with a few drops of sesame oil.

2 sliced zucchini (any color or a combination)
1 large yellow onion
1 small scallion
4 cloves garlic
4–5 stalks green onions
6 button mushrooms
1 large firm tomato
2 tablespoons toasted sesame oil
1 tablespoon seasoned rice vinegar
1 tablespoon Italian seasonings
½ teaspoon sea salt
½ teaspoon white pepper

Sliced vegetables 1/8 inch thick and place on aluminum foil top with herbs oil, and vinegar. Fold over, and fold all edges, sealing airtight. Place in the medium heat part of your barbeque grill and cook for 30 minutes. Slowly unwrap and check for desired tenderness (Steam can cause skin burns).

2 teaspoons dried basil
1 large dried bay leaf
1 teaspoon cayenne pepper
2 teaspoons brown sugar
4 cups chicken stock/broth
thickener such as flour, corn starch or arrow root

Sauté` all vegetables in oil until tender.
Add meats and dried spices, simmer for30 minutes over low heat.
Add remaining ingredients and simmer for an additional 30 minutes.
Thicken with a thickening agent to a chili like consistency, simmer for 15 minutes.
Garnish with a dabble of minced onion and parsley on top.
Serve with fresh warm corn bread and a pat of butter.

Dennis' Super Mashed Potatoes

This is a recipe I have altered from as old Irish potato dish called Colcannon Potatoes. I have added a few more delicate vegetables and a few strips of bacon for flavor. This version of mashed potatoes will make your dinner guests or family screaming for more, so make extra!

6 large Idaho potatoes
6 medium red potatoes (leave the skins on)
1 stick (¼ cup) butter
¼ cup olive oil
½ cup cream (milk is fine)
1 medium coarsely chopped carrot
1 large sliced onion
4 chopped cloves of garlic
½ medium sliced cabbage
4 slices slivered bacon

Prepare the potatoes as you would for basic mashed potatoes, (potatoes, milk/cream & butter).
Sliver the bacon and sauté over medium flame until tender
Add the onions, carrots and garlic until tender. Set aside.
Sauté the cabbage in olive oil until tender, add the other vegetables and heat together.
Spoon into the now mashed potatoes and mix well over low heat.
Top with dried chives for garnish.

Dennis' Sweet Potato Custard

A delightful light, flavorful sweet potato side that enhances any meal. It is superb, how the hint of banana makes this dish so enjoyable. Make extra, your guests will come back for more.

2 cups mashed cooked sweet potatoes
1 cup mashed bananas
2 cups evaporated milk
4 tablespoons packed brown sugar
4 egg yolks, beaten
1 teaspoon salt
½ cups raisins
2 tablespoons white sugar
2 teaspoons ground cinnamon

In a medium bowl, stir together the potatoes and bananas.
Add milk continue to stir and blend well.
Add brown sugar, egg yolk, and salt, mix thoroughly.
Spray a one quart casserole with non stick cooking spray.
Transfer mixture into the casserole dish.
Combine raisins, sugar and cinnamon; sprinkle over top.
Bake in a preheated 300 degree oven for 45 – 50 minutes or until a knife inserted near the center comes out clean.

Robin's Candied Yams

Every holiday the family gathers around the table for dinner. I will never forget the smiles on even the older guests when Robin places a large platter of the sweet mound on the dinner table.

1lb. unsalted butter
2lbs. sweet potatoes, cooked firm, peeled and sliced
2 cups packed brown sugar
2 sticks cinnamon
1 tablespoon vanilla extract

Heat the butter in a large fry pan.
Add vanilla extract.
Mix the dry ingredients together.
Coat the bottom of the pan with the dry ingredients and place the sliced potatoes in the pan,
turning when the potatoes receive a sugar coating.
Flip one time on each side.
Allow to cool before serving.
Makes 10-12 servings

I Have No Idea What to Call It Noodle Dish

Friday night, everyone is working late, and on their own providing dinner for themselves. Searching in the fridge and began to put this concoction together. I surprised myself and others who stopped over. I like it with a grilled main entrée; I suggest serving it with a delicate flavored meat such as grilled chicken breast, or a mild fish. The sour cream gives to dish a tart, yet not overpowering flavor.

2 lbs. cooked spiral pasta
3 large eggs
1 (8 oz.) container sour cream
1 medium chopped onion
3 cloves crushed garlic
½ chopped red bell pepper
4 leafs fresh basil
Few sprigs fresh rosemary
Olive oil

Over a medium heat sauté in olive oil, the red pepper, onion and garlic until tender.
Toss in the fresh herbs, sauté until tender.
Lower the heat and carefully move all the contents of the pan to the edge allowing the center of the pan to be empty.
Crack the eggs in the center, and beat them to a scrambled egg consistency.
Mix the entire contents together gently, bring to a simmer.
Add the sour cream
This dish can be served as a vegetarian dish or as a side.

Robins Grilled Potatoes and Onions

When the family is together on the weekends, we usually share the cooking chores. My wife Robin usually prepares the vegetables and I do the main course. In the summer we grill outdoors often. She puts together a easy and quick vegetable combination that is full of flavor and goes well with everything. If our daughters finish them without a fuss, then we know we did good!

4 large diced potatoes cleaned, unpeeled
2 large diced Vidalia onions
4 stalks sliced green onions
½ tablespoon garlic powder
½ tablespoon while pepper
1 tablespoon course kosher salt
2 tablespoons parmesan cheese
Several pats of butter
Fresh rosemary, thyme, or dill when available. Try not to use dried.

Place vegetable on an aluminum foil sheet, top with the fresh herbs.
Top with pats of butter.
Fold over, including edges so that an airtight pouch is formed.
Place in top rack of a barbeque grill and cook until potatoes are tender.
Make sure once you have checked the vegetables, you reseal the pouch airtight, so that no steam is lost.

Candied Yams – Lionel Gemus

1lb. unsalted butter
2lbs. sweet potatoes, peeled and coarsely chopped
2 cups sugar
1 cup water
1 cup packed dark brown sugar
2/3 unpeeled orange, sliced and seeded (stem slice discarded)
2/3 unpeeled lemon, sliced and seeded (stem slice discarded)
2 sticks cinnamon
1 tablespoon vanilla extract
½ teaspoon ground mace

Heat butter in a 4 quart saucepan over high heat; when about half melted, add the remaining ingredients. Stir, cover and cook over high heat until mixture comes to a strong boil, about 10 minutes. Stir, and then reduce heat and simmer covered for 20 minutes. Uncover and continue cooking until sweet potatoes are very tender, about 20 minutes, stirring occasionally. Remove from heat and discard cinnamon sticks. Serve immediately, un-drained.
Makes 10-12 servings

Potato Lasagna

Don't be scared of the name. I can't think of any other was to describe my dish of potatoes and cheeses in layers, so this is what I have decided to call my dish. The recipe consists of layers of potatoes between layers of cheeses, spices, and herbs. I allowed my toughest critic, my mother to be the first to try this recipe. After asking for seconds, I knew it was right. This is a large amount; I suggest using this recipe when you are entertaining a small party of 8 – 12 guests. Otherwise cut the recipe in half. This can be used as a vegetarian dish.

3 medium peeled and thin sliced russet potatoes
3 medium peeled and thin sliced California gold potatoes
4 medium not peeled and thin sliced red potatoes
1 lb. Velveeta cheese
1 lb. cottage cheese (small curd)
½ lb. mozzarella cheese
½ cup grated parmesan cheese
½ cup sliced green onions
2 teaspoons granulated garlic
season salt to sprinkle
white pepper to sprinkle
1 cup Italian bread crumbs
Olive oil

Save1/3 the amount of each of the potatoes, and set aside.
In a large frying pan, coat the bottom with a thin layer of olive oil.
Arrange a layer of russet potatoes, drizzle with a small amount of olive oil.
Top with salt, pepper, mozzarella cheese.
Another layer of California gold potatoes, drizzle with a small amount of olive oil.
Top with granulated garlic, cottage cheese, small amount of bread crumbs.
Another layer of red potatoes, drizzle with a small amount of olive oil.
Top with salt, pepper, Velveeta cheese (in thin pencil like slices).
The last layer of a menagerie of the 1/3 potatoes which was set aside.
Top with olive oil, onions, parmesan cheese, and bread crumbs.
Cover (I use aluminum foil) and fry over a low flame until the bottom layer begins to brown (approx. 35 – 40 minutes).
Remove from stove and place into a broiler over medium high heat until the top layer browns (approx. 6 – 10 minutes).
Serve hot.

Dennis' Red Beans and Rice

In this recipe, I think I have mastered the combination of meats, beans, and rice. The flavor explodes on your palette, leaving a flavor of sweet, salt and smoke. The only other requirement is a square of fresh, warm, corn bread.

2 lbs. ground beef
2 chopped onions
5 cloves chopped garlic
2 celery stalks
1 Hungarian hot pepper
1 chopped green bell pepper
1 lb. cubed smoked or Polish sausage or
1 lb. cubed bratwurst (I sweat it over low heat first to remove most of the grease) or
1 lb. cubed Andouille sausage (I sweat it over low heat first to remove most of the grease)
¼ cup liquid smoke
¼ cup corn syrup
¼ cup vegetable oil
1 teaspoon dried oregano
2 teaspoons dried basil
1 large dried bay leaf
1 teaspoon cayenne pepper
2 teaspoons brown sugar
4 cups chicken stock/broth
Thickener such as flour, corn starch or arrow root

Sauté` all vegetables in oil until tender
Add meats and dried spices, simmer for30 minutes over low heat
Add remaining ingredients and simmer for an additional 30 minutes
Thicken with a thickening agent to a chili like consistency, simmer for 15 minutes
Garnish with a dabble of minced onion and parsley on top
Serve with fresh warm corn bread and a pat of butter

Main Entrée's

In the following eight sections, you will find an abundant amount of entrees allowing you to choose which meat you prefer. Beef/Veal, Game, Lamb, Pork, Poultry, Seafood, & Vegetarian.

Beef & Veal

Here are some of my favorite beef & veal recipes

Dennis' Maltese Beef Olives - (Bragjoli)

This is a time consuming recipe well worth the effort. I like to invite friends over for this meal, just to watch there reaction from the first bite. This is definitely a meal to be served on special occasions or when impressing a loved one.

3 lbs. four slices of very thin steak (I use flank)
¾ lb ground meat (pork and beef mixed) OR diced ham (traditional)
2 cans tomato sauce
1 large chopped onion
4 cloves chopped garlic
½ cup grated parmesan cheese
2 sprigs Italian parsley
1 sprig marjoram
1 teaspoon each salt fresh ground pepper
3 teaspoons olive oil
3 chopped hard boiled eggs
1 cup red wine

In a large skillet:
 Saute' the ground meat with half the onion and garlic in the olive oil cooking until the meat is medium rare.
Remove from heat and drain off excessive grease fro the meat, cool to room temperature
Add eggs and cheese, mix well
Carefully place ground meat mixture in individual steak pieces and roll up, tucking in the ends and tie up with string.

Place in a baking dish:
Add wine tomato sauce and remaining onions and garlic, cover and bake in the oven at 350 degrees for 45 minutes or until the outer layer of steak in tender. Uncover and bake an additional 15 minutes. Serve with boiled potatoes, onions, and carrots drizzled with olive oil and fresh Italian or Maltese bread.

Beef Wellington - Lionel Gemus

If Goose liver is not one of your favorite flavors, omit it. I have done this when I myself. This recipe is well worth the effort. The flavor will be one your guests will never forget.

4lb. fillet of beef, trimmed of all fat and skin, and trussed for roasting.
¼ cup pure vegetable oil
2 cups coarsely chopped onions (2 large)
1 cup sliced celery
½ cup dry sherry Madeira
2 can (10 ½ oz each) beef broth
1 tablespoon cornstarch
1 tablespoon water
¼ cup minced shallots or green onions
¼ cup butter or margarine
1 lb. mushrooms very finely diced
½ teaspoon salt
   dash pepper
4-5 tablespoons pate or puree of goose liver pastry for 2 pie crusts
     (I use puff pastry and butter to replace the pate)
1 large egg yolk
1 tablespoon water

Heat the oil in a roasting pan over medium heat, add the filet, brown it on all sides, then remove it and set it aside to cool for one hour. The onions and celery are added to the fat remaining in the roasting pan and are cooked until they are slightly colored.

The fat in the pan is poured off and the sherry or Madeira is added very carefully. Cook for one minute. The beef broth is added and the mixture brought to a boil. Blend 1 tbsp of water with the cornstarch, stir it into the mixture in the pan and continue the stirring until the sauce has thickened. The sauce is allowed to simmer 10-15 minutes, the seasoning is corrected, and the sauce is strained and set aside until ready to heat and serve.

To make the filling-cook the shallots or green onions 2 minutes in the butter or margarine in a large skillet over medium heat. Add the mushrooms salt and pepper and cook 7-8 minutes or until all the moisture disappears, stirring occasionally. Turn the mixture into a bowl and stir in the goose liver. Taste and correct the seasoning and cool 1 hour.

Prepare your pastry or puff pastry. Turn it out on a lightly floured surface and roll it out to a rectangle 3-4 inches longer than the filet and wide enough to encase it

(continued)

To assemble, spoon about a third of the mushroom mixture down the center of the pastry rectangle. Untruss the fillet and place it over the mushroom mixture, then spool the rest of the mixture onto the fillet, patting it in place, if necessary. Bring one side of the pastry up and over the filet, then lift and bring the opposite side up and over. Moisten the long edge and press it firmly. The ends are moistened, tucked in, and pressed together to seal firmly closed. Pick up the filet with both hands and place it on an ungreased cookie sheet with the seam side down to let the steam escape during baking, make a small hole in each end two or three on top.

Cut designs from the pastry scraps, and moisten them and arrange on the filet.
At this point if you like, you may cover the filet with aluminum foil and refrigerate overnight. If you do, let it stand at room temperature for 20 minutes before baking.

Just before baking, beat the egg yolk and 1 tbsp of water and brush it over the pastry and designs, bake at 425 degrees for 30 minutes.
Remove it from the cookie sheet carefully with 2 broad spatulas and let it stand 10 minutes before slicing.

Heat the wine sauce and serve it in a sauceboat.
Makes 6-8 servings, if you aren't hungry.

Beef Burgundy

This is one of the old school recipes. Everyone has heard of this meal, but I don't think anyone has ever made it. The family enjoys this beef dish with a hint of sweetness from the wine. The best part is that is seem to be a high class meal, but you are using a mid-priced cut of meat.

2 tablespoons vegetable oil
1 – 1 ½ lbs. beef round steak cubed into 2 inch cubes
2 medium onions sliced
2 cloves garlic crushed
4 oz. button mushrooms halved
1½ cup dry red wine
1 tablespoon tomato paste
1 bay leaf
2 teaspoons Worchester sauce
2/3 cup pitted prunes
1 tablespoon cornstarch
sea salt
white pepper
water

Preheat over to 325 degrees.
In a large skillet heat the oil over medium heat. Add beef, sauté until browned.
Add onions and garlic and stir, cook for 10 minutes.
Transfer to a 3 quart (large) casserole dish, and set aside.
Add wine to the same skillet and bring to a slow boil.
Stir in the tomato paste, bay leaf , Worchester sauce and prunes.
Season with salt and pepper.
Pour mixture over beef, cover and bake for 2 hours.
In a small bowl, blend cornstarch with a small amount of cool water, and add to the casserole dish.
Remove the bay leaf and gently stir. Bake for an additional 20 minutes

Dennis' Hungarian Beef Goulash

This is the real recipe for Hungarian Beef Goulash. Most people think that beef goulash is made of macaroni and beef with a few other spices, wrong! Beef Goulash is a sort of a beef stew with dumplings.

2 pounds beef chuck, cut into 2-inch cubes, patted dry
kosher salt, as needed, plus 1 tablespoon
freshly ground black pepper
flour for dredging
vegetable oil for searing, plus 3 tablespoons
1 large yellow onion, thinly sliced
4 cloves garlic, minced
2 teaspoons sweet paprika
1 teaspoon hot paprika
1 teaspoon caraway seeds
2 cups whole, peeled, canned tomatoes (with puree), roughly chopped
4 cups cold water
3 sprigs flat-leaf parsley
3 sprigs fresh thyme
1 bay leaf
3 tablespoons sour cream, plus more for the table

Serving suggestion: BUTTERED EGG NOODLES WITH PARSLEY, recipe follows, rice, or sauerkraut.

Spread the beef out on a baking sheet and season generously with salt and pepper. Dredge the beef in the flour. Transfer the beef to a fine mesh strainer and shake off any excess flour.
Heat a large Dutch oven with a tight-fitting lid over high heat. Pour in enough oil to reach about 1/3 of an inch up the sides. Add half of the beef and cook, uncovered, stirring occasionally, until well-browned, about 6 minutes. Using a slotted spoon, transfer the beef to a plate, leaving the oil in the Dutch oven. Repeat with the remaining beef. Drain the oil and wipe out the pan.
Preheat the oven to 275 degrees F. Return the Dutch oven to medium-high heat, and add the remaining 3 tablespoons oil. Sauté the onion, stirring, until lightly browned, about 5 minutes. Add the garlic, paprika, and caraway and cook, stirring, until fragrant, about 1 minute. Add the tomatoes and simmer, stirring, until thickened, about 2 minutes more. Add the beef and water, cover, and bring to a boil. Using a piece of kitchen twine, tie together the parsley, thyme, and bay leaf and add to the pot. Braise in the oven, covered, until the beef is tender, about 1 1/2 hours.

(Continued)

Remove from the oven and set aside for 5 minutes. Skim the fat from the surface of cooking liquid with a ladle. Bring to a simmer, uncovered, on top of the stove, stirring occasionally, until liquid has thickened, about 20 minutes. Stir in the sour cream and continue to simmer, stirring occasionally, until the liquid has reduced to a sauce-like consistency and the beef is very tender, about 20 minute more. Stir in the remaining 1 tablespoon salt and season with pepper to taste. Remove and discard the herb bundle.

Divide among bowls and serve with BUTTERED EGG NOODLES WITH PARSLEY, rice, or sauerkraut. Pass sour cream at the table.

Cook's Note: Beef chuck is the choice for any type of stew. If you can't find chuck cubed for stew in your meat department, buy a thick steak and cut it into 2-inch cube it yourself.

BUTTERED EGG NOODLES WITH PARSLEY

12 ounces wide egg noodles
6 tablespoons unsalted butter, cut into small pieces and chilled
3 tablespoons minced flat-leaf parsley leaves
1/4 teaspoon kosher salt, plus more as needed
freshly ground black pepper
1/4 teaspoon grated lemon zest (optional)

Bring a large pot of water to a boil and salt generously. Add the noodles and cook until al dente, tender but not mushy.

Meanwhile, ladle 1/4 cup of the noodle cooking water into a medium skillet. Set the skillet over low heat and, while whisking constantly, gradually add the butter, piece by piece, (let each piece of butter melt into the sauce before adding the next bit) until a smooth sauce has formed. Stir in the parsley and season with salt and pepper to taste. Add the lemon zest if desired.

Drain the noodles in a colander in the sink and leave whatever water clings to them--do not rinse. Transfer the noodles to a large bowl, add the sauce, and toss until well-coated. Serve.

Yield: about 4 to 6 side dish servings.

Dennis' Grape Leaves

The best I have ever had. This recipe can be used as a main entrée, or as an appetizer, It can also be served warn or cold. I enjoy grape leaves for breakfast right out of the refrigerator.

1 pound ground beef (lamb may be used, I prefer beef. Lamb is to strong)
3/4 cup uncooked white rice
1 teaspoon garlic powder
2 teaspoons allspice
1/2 teaspoon salt
1/2 teaspoon pepper
1/2 teaspoon ground cinnamon
1 jar grape leaves, or about 50 fresh grape leaves
1/4 cup olive oil
1 pound pork or lamb chops
1 tomato, sliced
1/2 cup lemon juice
40 garlic cloves

In a large mixing bowl, mix together the ground beef, rice, garlic powder, allspice, salt, pepper, and cinnamon, and set aside.
Rinse grape leaves several times. If the leaves are small, leave them intact, but cut out the large center vein. If the leaves are large, cut them in half vertically, cutting out the large vein in the process.
Place a small amount of the ground meat mixture at the end of each leaf. Roll up egg-roll style.
Pour the oil into the bottom of a large Dutch oven. Lay the chops over the oil. Lay the tomato slices over the chops.
Place the stuffed grape leaves seam-side down on top of the chops. Pack the leaves tightly and begin a second layer when necessary.
Place whole garlic cloves randomly between the rolled leaves; plenty of garlic on each layer.
When you are done stacking, pour the lemon juice over the leaves, and add water to the pot to about 2-inches above the rolled leaves. To prevent the leaves from unrolling during cooking, place a plate on top of the stack of leaves and place a heavy object on top of the plate.
Simmer the leaves over low heat for about 2 hours.
Invert the entire Dutch oven into a large platter with high sides (i.e. a 12-inch round cake pan). Or, remove the leaves from the pot with tongs. Serve rustic style, with plenty of Arabic bread on which to spread the garlic!

Beef Bourguignon - Lionel Gemus

This recipe is absolutely phenomenal. After the time and effort, it is well worth it. I enjoyed the recipe so much; I served the following weekend for friends. I left it in the exact format I received it in to make the steps easier to follow.

Preheat oven to 450 degrees use a cast iron cooking pot or   fireproof casserole. The cast iron cooking pot with heavy cover gives the most satisfactory result in making this dish.

60z. chunk of bacon 1tbsp oil (olive or cooking)	Cut into pieces ¼" thick and long 1 1/2" long. Sautee in oil over moderate heat for 3 minutes to brown slightly. Remove with slotted spoon and set aside temporarily.
3lbs stewing beef Cut into 1 1/2" cubes (Sirloin tip is the best For this purpose)	dry beef with paper towels to facilitate browning. Sautee beef (in small portions) in bacon and oil mixture until nicely browned on all sides. Set aside with the bacon until all the beef is browned.
2 sliced carrots 2 small sliced onions	Sautee onions and carrots until onions are slightly browned. Remove all grease that may be left in the pot. Return beef and bacon to pot/casserole.
1tsp salt ¼ tsp fresh ground pepper 2tbsp flour	Toss beef with salt and pepper and sprinkle with flour. Toss again to give it a coating. Place pot uncovered in middle position of pre-heated oven for 4 minutes. Toss meat again and return to oven for another 4 minutes. (This browns the flour and covers the meat with a light crust.) Remove iron pot or casserole from oven. Turn oven down to 325 degrees.

(Continued)

¼ cup warm brandy

pours brandy over meat and ignites with match

3 cups dry red wine
2 or three cups canned

stir in wine and enough consommé to barely cover meat. Add tomato paste, garlic, and herbs. Bring to a simmer on top of stove.

Beef consommé (or
Substitute 2 0r 3 cups
Made with beef cubes)
1bsp tomato paste
3 cloves mashed garlic
½ tsp thyme
I crumbled bay leaf
(Continued)

Cove pot and set on lower third of pre-heated oven (325 degrees). To start, periodically lift top to check and regulate oven heat so liquid simmers very slowly for 3-4 hours. Meat is done when very tender and fork pierces it easily. Season with salt and pepper to taste.

Meanwhile, while the meat is cooking, prepare the mushrooms and onions.

18-24 small onions
1-1/2 tbsp butter
1-1/2 tbsp oil
9-10 inch skillet

when butter and oil are bubbling in skillet, add onions and Sautee over moderate heat for about 10 minutes. Roll the onions about to brown them as evenly as possible. You cannot expect to brown the uniformly.

(Continued)

12oz. fresh mushrooms

Washed and well dried.
Left whole if small, or
Cut in quarters if large.
2tbsp butter
1tbsp oil
10-inch skillet.

Place skillet over high heat. As soon as you can see the butter foam has begun to subside, add mushrooms, a few at a time. They should not be crowded to avoid steaming. After 3-4 minutes the will begin to brown. Remove immediately from the skillet.

When meat is tender, distribute onions and mushrooms over the meat and simmer for approximately 4 minutes. Skim any obvious fat from the top. The sauce should be approximately 2 ½ cups, thick enough to coat a spoon lightly. If too thick add liquids or boil it down if too thin. Season to preferred taste. Serve from casserole or serving platter.

Serves 6

Lemon veal – Lionel Gemus

I will admit, I have not tried this recipe, but I do trust my friend Mike, Lionel's son. He explained to me that it is a very flavorful dish, allowing the veal not to be over poweded, with a faint hint of lemon.

1½ lb veal cutlets (not necessarily milk fed, the lesser expensive is okay)
3 tablespoons oil
1 sheet of plastic wrap
salt and pepper
flour for dredging

Large iron skillet
Wooden mallet

1 preparation of lemon butter sauce (see recipe)

Place individual cutlet on cutting board or other flat surface. Cover with plastic wrap and flatten each side evenly to 1/8" with a wooden mallet. Salt and pepper to taste.

Dredge the veal cutlets in flour and shake off excess. Heat skillet on medium high heat and when heated, pour in oil and sauté veal until brown approximately 2 minutes on each side.

In warm serving platter pour some of the reserved lemon sauce and roll the cutlets in it. Pour some more of the lemon sauce over the veal. Garnish with chopped parsley and serve immediately.

Loraine's Smothered Steak

When I began to cook at my deli/soul food carry out in downtown Detroit, I hired my good friend Loraine she explained to me that if you want to cook good soul food, "ya gotta put grandma's toe in it" I remember her standing next to me until she was satisfied of the result of her old family recipes. Lorraine was born and raised in Mississippi, and this recipe is as southern as it can get.

4 – 6 medium thick round, chip, or flank steak
2 large beaten eggs
2-1 cup milk portions
2 large thin sliced onions
3 cloves chopped garlic
3 cups all purpose flour
1 teaspoon garlic powder
1 teaspoon sugar
2 teaspoons paprika
1 tablespoon seasoning salt
1 teaspoon pepper
1 - 2 cups canola oil

Prepare an egg wash with the milk and eggs
Combine all the dry ingredients in a bowl, mix well
Dip the steaks in egg wash, then placing in the breading and fry until medium rare, save the remaining breading for later.
Once finished frying, remove the steaks, set aside, and add the onions and garlic fry until tender, yet still firm.
Remove as much onion and garlic as possible and set aside.
Cool the oil down to room temp., add the milk and flour used for breading, stirring slowly to remove any lumps.
Bring to a simmer, keep adding flour, slowly stirring, until a loose gravy has been formed.
Place ½ the gravy at the bottom of a baking dish, place the steaks on top, then the onions and topping it off with the remaining gravy. (Make sure the chops are completely submerged in the gravy)
Cover and bake at 300 degrees for 45 minutes.
Serve with white rice and a green vegetable.

Maltese Stuffed Eggplant (Bringiel Mimli)

Growing up in Corktown, My Nana always made the dish in the summer, when the eggplant was always available. My Grandfather (Nunu) would grow them in his garden. I enjoyed growing up in Corktown with my grandmother's cuisine, she taught me so much. I give her most of the credit for making me so interested in cooking.

1 large eggplant
1 lb. ground beef
1 medium onion-chopped
1 tablespoon tomato paste
1 teaspoon grated cheese
   dash of allspice
   dash of marjoram
   salt and pepper to taste

Cut the eggplant in half, longwise. Place in a pot of water and boil about 10 minutes. Remove the eggplant from water. Spoon out the center and chop ½ the center into small pieces.

In a large bowl, put beef, onion, egg, tomato paste, eggplant centers, cheese, spices. Mix well. Fill the eggplants evenly with meat mixture. Place the stuffed eggplants in a roasting pan. Add a little water and bake covered, for 1-1/2 hours at 350.

Whole potatoes, carrots and onions may be put into the roasting pan and cooked along with the eggplant for a complete dinner.

Nana's Corned-Beef Torta

This is very similar to a beef torta. Yet, it has a very nice flavor, since the recipe calls for replacing the beef with corned beef from a can. DO NOT use fresh corned beef; it is much to tart and firm. From what I unruffled, back during the wars, Malta had problems getting beef to the market, so the Maltese community replaced it with canned corned beef (called Bulibif pronounced-bul li' beef). Some Maltese cooks (my father one of them) mixed the ground beef with canned corned beef. It tasted great, but I like it better using just corned beef. It also is a nice touch adding the cubed potatoes. This distinguishes it from a beef torta.

The trick is not to add the corned beef until the very last 15 minutes allowing the meat to warm a bit; otherwise the corned beef will melt and disintegrate into the sauce.

For the crust, use the recipe in this book.

1 pie crust (top & bottom)
1 lb. canned corned beef
2 medium potatoes cubed very small
1 medium chopped yellow onion
4 cloves crushed garlic
½ cup green peas (I prefer frozen)
1 tablespoons tomato paste
4 tablespoons olive oil
1 teaspoon curry powder (optional)
1 teaspoon sea salt
1 teaspoon white pepper
1 teaspoon Italian seasonings

In a frying pan, brown in olive oil, the onions and garlic together.
Add Potatoes and simmer 15 minutes. Careful not to damage during stirring.
Add the tomato paste, dry spices, simmer and additional 20 minutes.
If the mixture seems to be drying out, add a ¼ cup at a time of warm water.
Add the corned-beef, and bring down to a slow simmer.
Toss in the Peas and cook just until the peas are warm.

Roll out the crust, and spread the crust over a pie pan and fill with
the meat filling.
Top off the pie and with a fork, press the edges sealing the pie.
Poke 5 holes in the top of the crust.
If preferred. For a more rich, brown crust, lightly, brush the
top with a beaten egg.
Bake in a pre heated 350 degrees oven until the crust turns deep golden brown.

Nana's Maltese Beef Torta

Beef Torta is a Maltese ground beef pie. It may appear like a huge pot pie, but it has a totally different taste including the crust, it has a more flaky crust with a "sweeter" taste. My Nana (Grandmother) would serve these pies with different filling. It is sort of in-between an appetizer and a main course. The Maltese serve this when company is over visiting. Not a meal, nor just a snack. Torta goes well anytime, I have enjoyed it from breakfast to a midnight snack.

For the crust, use the recipe in this book.

1 pie crust (top & bottom)
1 lb. ground beef
1 medium chopped yellow onion
4 cloves crushed garlic
½ cup green peas (I prefer frozen)
2 tablespoons tomato paste
4 tablespoons olive oil
1 teaspoon curry powder (optional)
1 teaspoon sea salt
1 teaspoon white pepper
1 teaspoon Italian seasonings

In a frying pan, brown in olive oil, the onions and garlic together.
Add the ground beef, and bring down to a slow simmer.
Add the tomato paste, dry spices, simmer and additional 20 minutes.
If the mixture seems to be drying out, add a ¼ sup at a time of warm water.
Toss in the Peas and cook just until the peas are warm.

Roll out the crust, and spread the crust over a pie pan and fill with the meat filling.
Top off the pie and with a fork, press the edges sealing the pie.
Poke 5 holes in the top of the crust.
If preferred. For a richer, brown crust, lightly, brush the top with a beaten egg.
Bake in a pre heated 350 degrees oven until the crust turns deep golden brown.

Nana's Corned-Beef Torta

This is very similar to a beef torta. Yet, it has a very nice flavor, since the recipe calls for replacing the beef with corned beef from a can. DO NOT use fresh corned beef; it is much to tart and firm. From what I unruffled, back during the wars, Malta had problems getting beef to the market, so the Maltese community replaced it with canned corned beef (called Bulibif pronounced-bul-li'beef). Some Maltese cooks (my father one of them) mixed the ground beef with canned corned beef. It tasted great, but I like it better using just corned beef. It also is a nice touch adding the cubed potatoes. This distinguishes it from a beef torta.

The trick is not to add the corned beef until the very last 15 minutes allowing the meat to warm a bit; otherwise the corned beef will melt and disintegrate into the sauce.

For the crust, use the recipe in this book.

1 pie crust (top & bottom)
1 lb. canned corned beef
2 medium potatoes cubed very small
1 medium chopped yellow onion
4 cloves crushed garlic
½ cup green peas (I prefer frozen)
1 tablespoons tomato paste
4 tablespoons olive oil
1 teaspoon curry powder (optional)
1 teaspoon sea salt
1 teaspoon white pepper
1 Teaspoon Italian seasonings

In a frying pan, brown in olive oil, the onions and garlic together.
Add Potatoes and simmer 15 minutes. Careful not to damage during stirring.
Add the tomato paste, dry spices, simmer and additional 20 minutes.
If the mixture seems to be drying out, add a ¼ cup at a time of warm water.
Add the corned-beef, and bring down to a slow simmer.
Toss in the Peas and cook just until the peas are warm.

Roll out the crust, and spread the crust over a pie pan and fill with
the meat filling.
Top off the pie and with a fork, press the edges sealing the pie.
Poke 5 holes in the top of the crust.
If preferred. For a more rich, brown crust, lightly, brush the
top with a beaten egg.
Bake in a pre heated 350 degrees oven until the crust turns deep golden brown.

<u>Game</u>

Alligator, Duck, Pheasant, Rabbit, & Venison
Life's good!

Bavarian Venison

While watching a television show last winter, I tried this recipe. I cannot say anything bad. Even my mother didn't know what she was eating!

2 lbs. ground deer
2 eggs
1 teaspoon salt
½ teaspoon onion salt
1 teaspoon grated lemon rind
¼ cup nonfat dry milk
¼ water
¼ dry bread crumbs
1 tablespoon clarified butter
1 package beef gravy mix
3 tablespoons lemon juice
¼ cup brown sugar
¼ teaspoon ginger
3 whole cloves

In a large bowl, mix together the deer, eggs, salt, onion salt, lemon rind, dry milk, water and bread crumbs.
Shape into 8 patties about 1 inch thick.
In a skillet, melt a little butter over medium heat. Fry the patties until brown on both sides.
While the patties are cooking, prepare the gravy mix according to its directions.
To the gravy, add the lemon juice, brown sugar, ginger and cloves. Mix together.
When the patties are browned, pour the gravy over the patties.
Cover and simmer for 30 minutes basting several times.

Remove the cloves.

Bill's Hearty Venison Stew

I had a friend at work, he lived to hunt deer. This is his recipe.

1 (4lb) venison roast
2 tablespoons flour
1 can whole tomatoes, sliced
2 medium onions, sliced
1 cup water
2 cloves garlic
1 tablespoon garlic salt
½ teaspoon black pepper
¼ cup vinegar
¼ cup lemon juice
¼ cup ketchup
1 tablespoon Worcestershire sauce
2 tablespoons brown sugar
1 teaspoon prepared mustard
¼ teaspoon paprika

Rub flour into meat, brown well on all sides in a Dutch oven.
Add tomatoes, onions, water, garlic, garlic salt and pepper. Cover, simmer for 2 hours.
Combine remaining ingredients, pour over meat, cover and simmer until tender, 1 to 1 1/2 hours.

Crispy Duck

Easy and fast. This is a recipe for those who don't have all day to prepare a meal. This dish is absolutely delicious.

1 duck, domestic preferred
Kosher salt
pepper
Herbs de Province seasoning, found at most grocery stores

Remove most of the skin and fat. Render it down in a heavy pan over medium heat.
Cut duck into serving pieces; breast, legs, thighs.
Dry marinade overnight with Kosher salt, pepper and Herbs de Province.
In a skillet, sear duck, skin side down over high heat.
Put meat in a heavy baking pan. Add the duck fat.
Cover and bake at 250 degrees for 2 hours.

Dennis' Crock Pot Rabbit

I always thought one of the best kitchen tool, was the crock-pot. Many nights I have filled mine up, and placed it in the refrigerator for the next day's meal. This dish is at its best served over rice with a fresh green salad.

2 rabbits, cut into serving pieces
1 cup celery, sliced
1 cup carrots, peeled and sliced
1 onion, chopped
1 can water chestnuts, sliced
2 cups fresh mushrooms, sliced
3 cups chicken broth
Salt and pepper
2 tablespoons cornstarch
½ cup sherry

Place all ingredients except cornstarch and sherry in crock pot and cook on low for 6 hours.
Remove rabbit from pot.
In a separate bowl, combine sherry and corn starch.
Pour into crock pot to thicken the sauce.
Return rabbit to the crock pot and mix.
Serves 6-8

Dennis' Grilled Venison Steaks

I always asked for the back strap where the best steaks are at. When I put my hands on one, I would have the donor and a few friends over for a steak night and beer.

2 - 3 lbs venison steak
½ cups butter
¼ cups minced onion
2 teaspoons Worcestershire sauce
½ teaspoon dry mustard
½ teaspoon pepper

In a small saucepan, combine the butter, onion, Worcestershire, dry mustard & pepper.
Heat on low until the butter melts.
Brush the mixture on the steaks.
Grill steaks 15 minutes per side. Brushing the steaks with the butter mixture every time you turn.

Serve and Enjoy!

Dennis' Marinated Pheasant

Yogurt pulls out the wild game flavor. Makes a great meal during the hunt.

2 pheasants, cut into serving pieces
1 cup plain yogurt
½ teaspoon ground coriander seeds
1 tablespoon chili powder
¼ teaspoon pepper
½ teaspoon Dennis' season salt
1 teaspoon sugar
2 cloves garlic, crushed

In a bowl, mix the yogurt, coriander, chili powder, pepper, salt, sugar and garlic together.
Pierce the pheasant pieces all over with a fork.
Brush on the marinate and let it stand 45 minutes, brushing on more every 15 minutes.
Brush on another coating of the marinate and place the pheasant pieces on a broiling rack with foil under it.
Cook in the oven at 350 degrees for 30 - 45 minutes.
Serve with rice.

Dennis's Roast Pheasant

My friends would bring me back pheasant fro hunting trips. This is s nice and easy recipe to prepare you game bird.

2 - 3 pheasants
½ lemon
5 tablespoons butter
¾ cup raisins
juice of 3 oranges
1 teaspoon grated lemon rind
1 cup chicken broth, canned, homemade or made from bouillon
1/3 cup white wine
   salt and pepper

Rub the pheasants inside and out with the lemon. Salt and pepper inside and out to taste.
Put the pheasants in a baking dish breast up and spread on the butter.
In a bowl, mix the raisins, orange juice, lemon rind, chicken broth and wine.
Pour the broth mixture into the pan.
uncovered at 350 degrees for 45 minutes basting every 10 minutes.
Bake

Dennis' Rabbit Fricassee

Another WOW factor, serve this recipe to your guests, they will be surprised rabbit can taste this good. Serve with fried red skin potatoes on the side and fresh French garlic baguette.

2 cups red wine
2 tablespoons lemon juice
2 bay leaves
1 teaspoon thyme
¼ teaspoon marjoram
  salt and pepper
1 teaspoon garlic powder
2 rabbits, cut into serving pieces
2 tablespoons olive oil
1 onion, chopped
2 cloves garlic, minced
2 tablespoons cornstarch

Mix wine, lemon juice, bay leaves, thyme, marjoram, salt, pepper and garlic powder to make marinade. Place rabbit in large baking dish and pour marinade over rabbit.
Cover and refrigerate overnight. Remove rabbit from marinade when ready to cook and dry well. Strain marinade and save.
 Heat oil in a large skillet. Sauté onions and garlic.
Cover and simmer 1-1 ½ hours or until tender. Servings: 6-8

Dennis' Rabbit Pie

You have not savored a rabbit pie as this recipe. I have tried to accomplish the best recipe possible experimenting with different procedures, this it my favorite.

3 young rabbits
1 medium onion
5 rashers of un-smoked bacon
2 cloves of garlic
fresh herbs (rough chop parsley, thyme, chives, to taste)
small glass of dry sherry
frozen short crust pastry (unless you can make your own better)!
seasoning
1/2 pint whipping (heavy) cream

Place rabbits in a tray, whole and cover with bacon. Cook in moderate oven for about 15 minutes.
Meanwhile sweat sliced onions and crushed garlic in a pan until soft.
Add sherry and reduce.
When rabbits cooked, tear off as much meat as possible and add to pan with the bacon, chopped.
Toss in herbs; add a little water if necessary and cream.
Roll out defrosted pastry about 1/4 inch thick and egg wash.
Place rabbit mix in suitable pie dish and top with pastry.
Cook in moderate oven until pastry golden.
Pan fry kidneys in a little butter and serve as garnish.

Dennis' Venison Marsala

I really enjoy a good Marsala dish. One evening I thought why not? I prepared it the next day. Served it to my buddies during a ballgame.

4 venison chops
Cajun seasoning
2 tablespoons butter
3 tablespoons olive oil
¾ cup flour
¾ cup dry Marsala wine
¾ cup chicken stock
2 tablespoons butter, softened

Remove all fat and silver skin from the venison. Season with Cajun seasonings and let sit for 30 minutes.
Dredge in flour to coat and shake off excess flour.
Melt 2 tbsp butter and olive oil over medium heat in a large skillet.
When foam subsides, add meat and brown on both sides. Remove the chops and place on a warm plate.
Pour most of the fat off from the skillet. Add the wine and 1/4 cup of the stock. Bring to a boil over high heat for 2 minutes, scraping the bottom and sides of the skillet.
Reduce heat to low and add the venison back to the skillet and cook until medium rare, basting the meat with the sauce. Transfer the meat to a serving platter.
Add remaining 1/2 cup stock and any juices from the meat to skillet and bring back to a boil, scraping bottom and sides of skillet.
When sauce has reduced to a thick, syrupy consistency, remove from heat and season with salt and pepper to taste. Stir in 2 tbsp softened butter. Pour sauce over meat.

Manuel's Venison Stew

My dad's friends used to bring them cuts of venison. The only deal was when he were to prepare the venison, they came over for dinner.

2 lbs. venison, cut into bite size pieces
1 tablespoon olive oil
1 tablespoon garlic powder
1½ tablespoons onion powder
2 teaspoons Cajun seasoning
2 large onions, sliced into rings
1 cup fresh mushrooms
2 cans peas
4 - 5 large potatoes, cut into wedges (skin on if desired)
 carrots, as many as desired, skinned and cut into 2 inch pieces
1½ cups chopped celery
3 tablespoons browning sauce (Kitchen Bouquet)
3 beef bouillon cubes
1 cup red wine
1 tablespoon hot sauce
2 - 3 cups water
1½ cups all purpose flour

In a skillet, heat the oil. Add the deer. Season with the garlic powder, onion powder and Cajun seasoning to taste.
Lightly brown the meat. Drain off oil.
Place the meat in a large crock pot and add the other ingredients.
Cook on high for 2 to 3 hours stirring occasionally.
After the stew has cooked down after a few hours, slowly add the flour until the desired thickness of the gravy is achieved.
Turn crock pot to low and cook another hour. Stir every 15 minutes.

Serve with fresh bread and butter.

Rabbit Sauce Picante'

Rabbit does well in a Picante' sauce. This is s great recipe, using the freshest ingredients. Serve with a fresh green salad, crusty French baguette and a red wine.

1 large wild or tamed rabbit (cut in 8 pieces)
2 tablespoon butter
½ cup chopped onion
½ cup diced bell pepper
1 tablespoon sliced garlic
1 12oz can tomato paste
1 beef bouillon cube
2 cups beef or rabbit stock
1 cup all purpose flour
1 tablespoon lemon

Melt butter in black iron pot then dredge rabbit pieces in the 2 cups of flour.
Brown rabbits on all sides; next add onions, bell peppers, garlic, and sauté stirring in the vegetables thoroughly.
Turn heat to medium low, cover and simmer for 30 minutes, stirring occasionally.
Dilute beef cubes in hot water and add to beef or rabbit stock.
After simmering for 30 minutes add tomato paste and cook for 10 minutes, stirring often.
Add remaining flour to the pot and stir in well.
Cook for 5 minutes stirring very often.
Pour your liquid in gradually until reaching thickness desired (gravy should be like thick stew).
Add salt, red and black pepper to taste. I usually add 1/2 Tbsp of Worcestershire sauce and three dashes of, and add the lemon.
Serve with steamed rice garnished with fresh chopped parsley.

Reggie's Alligator Chili

You must try this recipe if you can purchase alligator meat. The humor alone knowing that your guests are eating alligator is great, but, don't allow the name to humor the flavor, it is a real winner.

3 pounds alligator meat, diced
½ cup oil
2 cups diced onions
1 cup diced celery
1 cup diced bell pepper
2 tablespoons diced garlic
2 tablespoons diced jalapenos
1 can (16 oz) pinto beans
3 cans (8 oz) tomato sauce
1 cup chicken stock
1 tablespoon chili powder
1 teaspoon cumin
salt and cracked black pepper to taste

In a heavy Dutch oven, heat oil over medium high heat. Add alligator and cook 20 minutes to render juices.
Add onions, celery, bell pepper, garlic and jalapenos. Sauté until vegetables are wilted, approximately 3 - 5 minutes.
Add pinto beans, tomato sauce and chicken stock. Bring to a low boil and reduce to simmer.
Add chili powder and cumin. Stir well.
Cook for 1 hour, stirring occasionally.
Once alligator is tender, season to taste using salt and black pepper.

This dish is always served at hunting camp dinners over spaghetti

Reggie's Alligator Jambalaya

A true Cajun recipe. I tried this several years ago, at a long lost friend of mine from the Bayou it was great.

1 lb. alligator meat, cut into 1/2 inch cubes
Cajun flavored marinate or your favorite flavor
1 lb. hot Italian sausage, cut into 1/2 inch chunks
3 tablespoons oil
2/3 cup chopped bell pepper
2 cloves garlic, minced
3/4 cup chopped parsley
1 cup chopped celery
2 cans (16oz.) tomatoes
2 cups chicken stock
1 cup chopped green onion
2 teaspoons oregano
1 tablespoon Cajun spice
1 teaspoon salt or to taste
2 cups cooked rice
Tabasco sauce

Place the alligator meat in a bowl with a lid and cover with the marinate. Refrigerate overnight. Drain when ready to use.
In a large pot, heat the oil over medium heat. Add the bell pepper, garlic, parsley and celery. Sauté until tender.
Add the tomatoes, chicken stock, onions, oregano, hot sauce, Cajun spice, salt, gator meat and sausage. Mix well.
Bring to a boil, reduce heat and simmer for 25 - 35 minutes or until the gator meat is done. Stir occasionally.
Serve over rice. Sprinkle with Tabasco sauce if desired.

Thai Curry Duck

This is the only way I enjoy duck. I always eaten duck greasy, not in this case. This recipe calls for a domestic duck, not a wild one.

1 medium size duck, cooked
2 large potatoes, cubed
1 stick butter
½ lb. mushrooms, quartered
¼ lb. small shallots, sliced in halves
2 cloves garlic, chopped
½ teaspoon pepper
1 package (3 oz.) Thai red curry paste
1 package (quart/liter) coconut milk/cream or two standard size tins
1 oz. coconut sugar (if not available, substitute honey)
1 oz. fish sauce
¼ cup finely chopped fresh sweet basil

Remove the duck meat from bone. Cut into bite size pieces.
Remove as much fat and skin as possible. If the skin is crispy and adhered to meat with a little fat, try to keep it intact.
Keep the fat and fatty skin. It will be used for flaming the curry.
Place in refrigerator.
Boil the potatoes to 80 % done. Drain and set aside.
In a skillet, sauté the mushrooms, shallots and garlic. Add pepper to taste.
Set aside.
In a skillet, add the duck fat and fatty skin to create oil. Remove the skin.
Add the curry paste and fry at medium heat, add additional oil if required.
Before the curry starts to burn add a few ounces of the coconut milk.
Let it thicken a bit. Keep stirring.
After a few minutes you will see the red oils slowly separating.
Stir in the coconut sugar/honey.
Stir in the fish sauce. Once it starts to thicken again, add the remaining milk.
Reserve an ounce or two.
Add the mushrooms, shallots and potatoes.
 Bring it to a low simmer for 10 minutes with the lid off.
Five minutes before serving add the sweet basil, duck and the rest of the milk.
Mix well and cover.
Served on rice accompanied by a cold beer,

Joe "Zepi's" Sautéed Rabbit

While visiting my lifelong friend Joe "Zepi" Troisi. He asked if I would stay fro dinner after he and his family just came home from a Maltese vacation. He brought back this recipe of rabbit prepared basically with wine and peas and he wanted a few of his friends to try it. Fried potatoes with garlic compliment this dish. It is out of this world.

1 Rabbit cut into 8 pieces
1 medium carrot coarsely chopped
2 medium sliced onions
6 cloves thin sliced garlic
2 cups frozen sweet peas
2 bay leafs
2 teaspoons sea salt
1 teaspoon black pepper
2 cups semi-sweet white wine
Olive oil

Prepare rabbit, rinse well and fry in olive oil until no blood
appears when stuck with a knife, set aside.
In the same pan without rinsing it, add a small amount
of oil, place over a medium flame.
Add the carrots, sauté 10 minutes.
Add garlic and onions, and bay leafs, sauté until the onions are transparent.
Place the rabbit over the vegetables, bring down to low heat.
Add peas and remaining ingredients; simmer very low for 1 hour,
while carefully stirring.

Note: Do not mix, just stir the bottom of the pan so it does not burn.

It is a nice compliment to fry cubed potatoes with a small amount of garlic powder on the side of this dish.

Lamb

Lamb can be a delicate to a very strong flavor. It depends what cut you are using. Be careful, and consider what the recipe calls for, some are for a delicate dish and others are for a more pungent meal.

Boneless Leg of Lamb with Grecian Stuffing

This lamb meal is easy. If you are familiar around the kitchen, you should have no problems. The recipe calls for light, yet aromatic flavors that will not over power the delicate taste of lamb.

3 tablespoons olive oil
6 cloves garlic, sliced thin lengthwise
½ cup cured black olives, chopped
¼ pound feta cheese, crumbled
½ cup sun dried tomatoes, packed in oil, chopped
4-5 pound boneless leg of lamb
1½ teaspoons crumbled dried rosemary
1 onion sliced
1 cup dry red wine
1½ cups beef broth
½ cup water
1 tablespoon cornstarch dissolved in 2 tablespoons cold water
Honey glazed baby carrots

Pat the lamb dry, arrange it, boned side up, on a work surface, and season it with salt and pepper, and rub with 2 tablespoons of oil.

Spread the lamb evenly with the olive-cheese-tomato mixture, leaving a 1-inch border around the edges.

Beginning with a short side, roll it up jelly roll fashion, and tie it tightly with kitchen string. The rolled and tied roast may look ungainly, but it will improve in appearance when cooked.

Transfer the lamb to a roasting pan and rub it all over with the remaining 1 tablespoon of oil, 1 teaspoon rosemary and salt and pepper to taste.

Roast the lamb in the middle of a preheated 325 degree oven for 30 minutes, scatter the onion around it in the pan, and roast the lamb for 1 to 1 1/4 hours more (a total of 20 minutes per pound of boneless meat) or until a meat thermometer registers 140 degrees for medium rare.

Transfer the lamb to a cutting board and let it stand for 20 minutes. While the lamb is standing, skim the fat from the pan drippings and set the roasting pan over moderately high heat, and add the wine, deglaze the pan, scraping up the brown bits, and boil the mixture until it is reduced by half.

Strain the mixture through a fine sieve into a sauce pan, add the broth, the remaining 1/2 teaspoon rosemary, the water, and any juices on the cutting board. Boil the mixture until it is reduced to about 2 cups.

Stir the cornstarch mixture, add it to the wine mixture, whisking, and simmer the sauce for 2 minutes.

Season the sauce with salt and pepper and keep it warm.

Discard the lamb strings.

Slice and arrange on a heated platter. Surround with clusters of the carrots. Strain the sauce into a heated sauceboat and serve with the lamb.

Lamb and Eggplant Pastitsio

If you have never had pastitsio before, you must give this dish a try. It is a delicate combination of flavorful layers that will melt in your mouth. Your guests will definitely cherish your effort. Ground beef may be substituted instead of the lamb.

For Lamb Sauce:
1 large onion, chopped
1 tablespoon extra-virgin olive oil
1 pound lean ground lamb
1 garlic clove, minced
1 1/2 teaspoons salt
1 teaspoon dried oregano, crumbled
½ teaspoon ground cinnamon
¼ teaspoon sugar
¼ teaspoon freshly ground black pepper
1 pound eggplant, peeled and cut into 1/2-inch cubes
1 (28 to 32-ounce) can crushed tomatoes

For Cheese Sauce:
2 tablespoons unsalted butter
2 tablespoons all-purpose flour
2 cups milk
1 garlic clove
1 whole clove
½ pound feta cheese, crumbled
½ teaspoon salt
¼ teaspoon freshly ground black pepper
2 large eggs

For Pasta:
10 ounces penne (3 cups)

To make lamb sauce: Cook onion in oil in a 4-quart heavy pot over moderately low heat, stirring, until softened, about 3 to 5 minutes.

Add lamb and cook over moderately high heat, stirring and breaking up lumps, until no longer pink, about 5 minutes.

Add garlic, salt, oregano, cinnamon, sugar, and pepper and cook, stirring, about 2 minutes.

Stir in eggplant and tomatoes and gently simmer, covered, stirring occasionally, until eggplant is just tender, about 40 minutes.

Remove lid and simmer, stirring occasionally, until sauce is thickened, about 15 minutes more.

Season with the salt and pepper.

(Continued)

Preheat oven to 425 degrees.

Make cheese sauce and cook pasta while lamb sauce is simmering:
Melt butter in a 2-quart heavy saucepan over moderate heat, then stir in flour and cook, stirring, for 2 minutes.
Whisk in milk and add garlic clove and whole clove, then bring to a boil, whisking constantly.
Reduce heat and simmer, whisking occasionally, for 5 minutes.
Add feta, salt, and pepper and cook, whisking vigorously, until cheese is well incorporated.
Beat eggs in a large bowl and gradually add sauce to eggs, whisking.
Cook pasta in a large pot of boiling salted water until just al dente, then drain in a colander. Toss half of pasta with lamb sauce and half with cheese sauce.

Assemble pastitsio:
Pour pasta with lamb sauce into a wide shallow 3-quart baking dish, spreading evenly.
Spoon pasta with cheese sauce on top, spreading evenly.
Bake pastitsio, uncovered, in middle of oven until bubbling and top is golden, about 25 to 30 minutes.
Let stand for 5 minutes before serving.

Marinated Grilled Lamb Kabobs

Finally a recipe that I have tried many times to enjoy enough to publish into my book. This is a typical kabob, with a light marinate.

Lamb and Marinade:
1 boneless leg of lamb (about 5 pounds)
½ cup extra-virgin olive oil
¼ cup lemon juice
¼ cup honey
6 cloves garlic, finely chopped
1 large white onion, finely chopped
¼ cup chopped fresh mint leaves
2 tablespoons chopped fresh oregano leaves
2 teaspoons chopped fresh rosemary leaves

Kabobs:
2 large white onions, cut into 2-inch squares
1 green bell pepper, cut into 2-inch squares
1 orange bell pepper, cut into 2-inch squares
1 red bell pepper, cut into 2-inch squares
1 yellow bell pepper, cut into 2-inch squares
1 pint cherry tomatoes, stemmed
1 (8-ounce) package white button mushrooms

Wooden skewers, soaked in water for 30 minutes

For the lamb: trim all fat from the lamb and cut into 2-inch cubes. Combine remaining marinade ingredients in a large re-sealable plastic bag and mix well.

Add the lamb cubes to the bag, tossing to coat. Seal bag and marinate in the refrigerator at least 2 hours, preferably overnight, rotating the bag occasionally to continually coat the lamb.

Preheat an outdoor grill to medium heat. Remove lamb from refrigerator about 30 minutes before grilling to bring the meat to room temperature.

To assemble the kabobs: fill skewers, alternating peppers, lamb, tomatoes, onions and mushrooms until all ingredients are used.

Grill skewers, rotating to char lamb on all sides, until cooked to desired doneness, about 7 to 8 minutes for medium-rare.

Dorothy's Moroccan Lamb Chops

When I first received this recipe from an old lady at one of my factories I deliver to at work, I was hesitant to try it. Easy and fast, a recipe that you can prepare after a days work and impress your dinner guests. It may be family or friends, they will not be disappointed.

1 pair of "frenched" lamb chops
1/3 cup apple cider
1 teaspoon brown sugar
Salt and freshly ground black pepper
2 cloves garlic, minced
1 pinch cinnamon
1 bosc pear, cored and cut into 6 wedges

Fried Plantains, recipe follows
Combine the apple cider, brown sugar, salt, freshly ground black pepper, garlic, and a pinch of cinnamon. For best results put in large resealable plastic bag. Add the lamb. Turn to coat the lamb. Squeeze out the air and seal the bag. Refrigerate for 30 minutes.

Preheat the oven to 350 degrees F.

Remove the lamb from the refrigerator and place in a roasting pan. Roast for 10 to 15 minutes (depending on temperature of meat preferred). Remove from oven and preheat the broiler.
Place 3 pear wedges on top of each piece of lamb. Place lamb under broiler for 2 to 3 minutes to allow the pears to caramelize with the brown sugar. Serve with Fried Plantains.

Fried Plantains:
Vegetable oil
2 green plantains, peeled, and sliced thinly lengthwise with a mandoline
Salt
Fill a deep pot halfway with oil. Heat the oil to 350 degrees F. Place plantains in hot oil and fry until golden and crisp. Remove to drain on a paper towel lined plate. Season immediately with salt.
Serve the plantains surrounding the lamb chops, over a bed of Jasmine rice.

North African Orange & Lamb Kebabs

I had this at a friends summertime gathering, just the right amount of herbs and spices, makes this recipe a well constructed meal. Serve with Jasmine rice and a fresh fruit salad for dessert.

½ cup loosely packed fresh cilantro leaves
½ cup loosely packed fresh parsley leaves
3 cloves garlic
1 teaspoon paprika
1 teaspoon ground cumin
½ teaspoon salt
¼ teaspoon freshly ground pepper
¼ cup nonfat plain yogurt
2 tablespoons lemon juice
1 pound lean leg of lamb
2 seedless oranges

Preheat grill to high.
Combine cilantro, parsley, garlic, paprika, cumin, salt and pepper in a food processor; process until the herbs are finely chopped.
Add yogurt and lemon juice; process until smooth.
Scrape into a medium bowl, add lamb and toss to coat.
Cover with plastic wrap and marinate in the refrigerator for 20 minutes.
Thread lamb and orange slices alternately onto 8 skewers.
Discard marinade.
Oil the grill rack
Grill the kebabs, turning occasionally, until cooked to desire doneness, 7 to 10 minutes for medium-rare.
Serve immediately.

Seared Petite Lamb Chops with Rosemary Balsamic Reduction

This is just what is says it is. Sweet, yet tangy balsamic sauce drizzled over young tender lamb chops. This is one of my favorite lamb dishes.

3 tablespoons extra-virgin olive oil
2 tablespoons finely chopped parsley leaves
1 tablespoon finely chopped rosemary leaves
1 teaspoon minced garlic
Kosher salt
6 (4-ounce) double lamb rib chops (2 ribs) with bones attached, ribs frenched
2 teaspoons freshly ground black pepper
1 tablespoon olive oil
2 tablespoons minced shallots
1 teaspoon minced garlic
1 cup balsamic vinegar
1 large or 2 small rosemary sprigs
2 tablespoons butter
Preheat the oven to 400 degrees F.

In a small bowl, combine olive oil, parsley, rosemary, and garlic. Season with salt, to taste. Set aside.

Set a 12-inch oven-safe sauté pan over medium-high heat. Season the lamb with 1 tablespoon of salt and 1 1/2 teaspoons of the black pepper. Add 1 1/2 teaspoons of the oil to the sauté pan and place the lamb, fat side down, in the pan. Sear the lamb until the fat has rendered and the skin is golden brown, about 3 minutes, and continue to cook the lamb, turning to cook evenly on each side, about 2 minutes each side. Baste them with the herb and oil mixture. Transfer the pan to the oven and cook until the lamb is rare, about 5 minutes. Alternatively, you can grill the lamb chops.

Make the balsamic drizzle while the lamb is cooking: Set a 1-quart saucepan over medium heat and add the remaining 1 1/2 teaspoons of olive oil. Once the oil is hot, add the shallots to the pan and sweat until translucent, about 1 minute. Add the garlic to the pan and sweat for 30 seconds. Pour the balsamic vinegar into the pan and bring to a boil. Add the rosemary and allow the balsamic to gently boil and reduce until only about 1/4 cup of balsamic remains, about 10 minutes. Season with 1 teaspoon of salt and 1/2 teaspoon of black pepper. Remove from the heat and swirl the butter into the pan. Remove the rosemary sprigs before using.

When the lamb is rare, remove from the oven and let rest for 5 minutes before serving. To serve, slice each double chop in half, and drizzle with the balsamic reduction.

Pasta & Rice

With new trendy restaurants emerging everyday, pasta and rice dishes have come out of their closets. Modern chefs are creating combinations that were never thought of. In this section I took that into perspective and came up with my favorite recipes.
Here are a few.

Aunt Carmen's Baked Rigatoni with Pork –
(Mqarrun Fil-Forn Bil Majjal)

I can remember as if it were yesterday. Aunt Carmen would walk into the front door at our house in Corktown on a holiday morning, the smile on her face lit the room, but the aroma of the dish she cradled so carefully in her arms was a sheer delight. Covered in a clean white towel, I could not wait to dig in. You'll enjoy this traditional Maltese dish as much as I still do.

2 lbs. lean ground beef or beef and pork
5-6 small pork chops or steaks
1 large chopped onion
4 cloves garlic
¼ cup olive oil
3 tablespoons cup tomato paste
2 cans tomato sauce
1 can crushed tomatoes
2 –3 fresh basil leaves
1 tablespoon oregano
4 oz. freshly grated parmesan cheese
6 eggs beaten
½ cup whole milk
2 lbs. cooked drained and chilled rigatoni pasta (store in cold water)
salt and pepper

Sauté in olive oil, onions garlic.
Add ground meat(s)
Sauté over medium heat with herbs and spices for 10 minutes
Add in tomato paste, bring down heat and stir for 2 – 3 minutes
so meat absorbs the paste
Once absorbed (will start to dry in approx. 5 minutes), add the tomato
sauce, crushed tomatoes, herbs and spices to taste.
Simmer for 1 hour on very low heat.
Chill to room temperature
Mix drained cold pasta with the milk, eggs and cheeses, saving
a small amount of the beaten eggs to brush with.
Roll out the dough and place in the bottom of a well-buttered baking dish
Place in the pasta and cover with the remaining dough, brush top with
eggs and place 6 small vents enabling steam to escape while cooking.
Bake at 325 degrees until tips of the pasta becomes dark brown.

Baked Macaroni Embedded in a Pastry Shell
(Timpana)

This is a very traditional Maltese entrée. I have had it several different ways, this is the most time consuming, but it is well worth the extra time put into it.

2 lbs. lean ground beef or beef and pork
½ lb. stewing beef
1 – 2 small Pork Steaks
1 large chopped onion
½ cup chopped bell pepper
4 cloves garlic
¼ cup olive oil
3 Tablespoons cup tomato paste
2 cans tomato sauce
1 can crushed tomatoes
2 –3 fresh basil leaves
1 tablespoon oregano
1 oz. freshly grated parmesan cheese
1 oz. grated Fontina cheese
6 large eggs beaten
½ cup whole milk
2 lbs. cooked drained and chilled Penne Pasta (store in cold water)
Salt and Pepper

2 ½ Basic Pastry Dough Recipes

Sliver both stewing beef and pork steaks and set aside.
Sauté in olive oil, onions garlic, green pepper.
Toss in slivered meats and cook until tender, add ground meat(s)
Sauté over medium heat with herbs and spices for 10 minutes
Add in tomato paste, bring down heat and stir for 2 – 3 minutes
so meat absorbs the paste
Once absorbed (will start to dry in approx. 5 minutes), add the
tomato sauce, crushed tomatoes, herbs and spices to taste.
Simmer for 1 hour on very low heat.
Chill to room temperature
Mix drained cold pasta with the milk, eggs and cheeses, saving a
small amount of the beaten eggs to brush with.
Roll out the dough and place in the bottom of a well-buttered
baking dish
Place in the pasta and cover with the remaining dough, brush
top with eggs and place 6 small vents enabling steam to escape
 while cooking.
Bake at 325 degrees until the crust is golden brown.

Dennis' Baked Rigatoni   (Imqarrun Fil-Forn)

I have experimented with this recipe many times. I found that it works best to mix the sauce with the pasta when they are cold, so that the eggs and cheese will cook along with the rest of the recipe in the oven, rather than on contact. You may omit the pork and even add other cuts of meat.

2 lbs. dried rigatoni noodles (Med.-Large Tubes)
1 small can tomato paste
2 cans tomato sauce
1 can stewed chopped tomatoes
1 ½ lbs. ground beef
½ lb. ground pork
1 large chopped onion
4 cloves chopped garlic
4 large eggs
1 teaspoon oregano
2 teaspoons basil
½ cup parmesan cheese
½ cup whole milk
¼ cup olive oil
1 teaspoon salt & pepper

Boil Macaroni in salted water, cook until just tender (Andante), chill under cold water.
In the olive oil, saute' the onions and garlic until tender
Add ground meat saute' until well done.
Remove any excess grease from the meat.
Add the tomato paste, mix well and saute' for 5 minutes.
Add tomato sauce and crushed tomatoes dried spices and simmer for 1 hour.
Cool down to room temperature.
Mix drained, cold pasta with the eggs, milk, salt and pepper.
Add the room temperature sauce and mix well, carefully not to damage pasta.
Bake in a 350 degrees oven for 1 hour or until the tips of the pasta becomes dark brown.
Serve with garlic bread and a simple salad.

Dennis' Baked Rice   (Ross Fil-Forn)

This also is a very traditional Maltese dish. When adding the eggs and baking, the results is a pudding like dish with a huge amount of flavor. Serve with a green salad, and crusty bread.

2 cups White rice (I use Jasmine)
1 small can tomato paste
2 cans tomato sauce
1 can stewed chopped tomatoes
1½ lbs. ground beef
½ lb. ground pork
1 large chopped onion
4 cloves chopped garlic
4 large eggs
1 teaspoon oregano
2 teaspoons basil
½ cup parmesan cheese
¼ cup olive oil
1 teaspoon salt & pepper

Boil rice in salted water, cook until just tender (Al' Dante), chill under cold water

In the olive oil, sauté' the onions and garlic until tender
Add ground meat sauté' until well done
Remove any excess grease from the meat
Add the tomato paste, mix well and sauté' for 5 minutes
Add tomato sauce and crushed tomatoes dried spices and simmer for 1 hour
Cool down to room temperature.
Mix drained, cold rice with the eggs, salt and pepper.
Add the room temperature sauce and mix well, carefully not to damage rice.
Bake in a 350 degrees oven for 1 hour.
Serve with garlic bread and a simple salad.

Dennis' Chicken Ravioli

Ravioli is a dish that can be stuffed with almost anything. I am fond of this chicken recipe. An Alfredo or basic tomato sauce both work well.

Pastry:
2 cups of flour
1 cup semolina or 1 egg slightly beaten
   dash of salt
   water as necessary to bind dough. let stand to room temperature

Filling:
1 lb. cooked chopped or ground chicken
1 medium minced onion
¼ cup heavy cream
2 cloves minced garlic
1 teaspoon Italian seasonings
1 tablespoon finely chopped Parsley
1 tablespoon grated cheese
   dash of salt

To make the pastry, mix flour, semolina or egg and salt. Add water
and work into a smooth dough. Rest the dough for one hour.

Prepare filling:
To make the filling, put all of the ingredients into a sauce pan and simmer on low heat until they are all combined together. Cool, place in a blender and blend until a thick and pasty consistency is acquired.

Divide Pastry into four pieces and roll into long strips about for inches wide. Dampen the edges with water. Put about one tablespoon of filling ¾ of and inch from the edge of the pastry and 1-1/2 inches apart. Turn one edge of pastry on the other one and press to seal.

Using a Ravioli cutter, cut the pastry ½ inch away from filling.
Set aside on a floured surface about 10 minuets. Boil in salt water in a large pot. In bottom of the pot place saucer upside down. This will prevent the Ravioli from sticking to bottom of pot.

Serve with tomato or Alfredo sauce* and grated parmesan cheese.

Dennis' Ham and Tortellini Pasta

I first tried this recipe in a quaint Italian restaurant. I came up with my rendition of this Dish. A sweet Alfredo sauce with ham and sweet peas to accompany this recipe. Best of all, full of flavor, as if you were cooking over a stove all day.

2 Lbs. tortellini (prepared Al Dente`)

For Sauce:
1½ lbs. cubed cooked ham
3 onions minced
1½ cups frozen sweet peas
6 cloves Garlic minced
1 teaspoon Allspice
2 teaspoons sugar
4 teaspoons olive oil
1 lb. parmesan cheese
1 lb. Asigio cheese
16 oz. heavy cream
whole milk
2 tablespoons cracked fresh pepper
2 cans chicken stock
2 teaspoons dried chopped parsley

Sautee` onions and garlic in the olive oil and add the chicken stock, bring to a boil.
Add the dry spices bring to a simmer.
At a very low heat add the heavy cream and stir in the cheeses.
Toss in Ham and peas
Once simmering, add milk to get to the right consistency you prefer.
Pour over tortellini and top with parmesan cheese.

Dennis' Special Pasta with Olive and Vegetables

This is made from a mistake. I served a few friends a couple of days before a spaghetti marinara, and in the fridge, I had a ton of boiled spaghetti pasta leftover without sauce. I was hungry and looking for a very quick light meal, I began to put this concoction together. I think it is one of the most tasteful light pasta meals in this book.

2 lbs. cooked (Al Dente`) spaghetti
1 medium minced onion
6 cloves chopped garlic
4 fresh X-large eggs
½ lb. chopped black and green olives
1 jar artichokes hearts (optional)
1 tablespoon tomato paste
¼ lb. sun dried tomatoes
¼ cup grated parmesan cheese
1 teaspoon sugar
salt & pepper to Taste
extra virgin olive oil

In a fry pan heat enough olive to cover entire bottom of pan about a ¼ of an inch
Drop the drained cold pasta in the pan and toss until warm
Crack the eggs, allow the white to roll down and begin to solidify, then crack the yolk and toss until the eggs are cooked
Add the tomato paste, toss until mixed well, and drizzle in another approx. ¼ cup olive oil
Add the remaining ingredients and toss until hot
Serve hot with hard crust bread

Four Cheese Stuffed Shells

Stuff shells are something everyone will enjoy. It is a real treat in the Spiteri household. The sauce is a sweeter sauce, without any meat. I take the time and add four cheeses to this recipe; it is well worth the time and effort. This may be used as a vegetarian dish.

Sauce:
2 (15 oz.) cans tomato sauce
1 (15 oz.) can crushed tomatoes
2 tablespoons tomato paste
¼ cup extra virgin olive oil
2 teaspoons sugar
1 tablespoon dries oregano
1 tablespoon dried basil
4 cloves crushed garlic
1 medium finely minced onion

Pasta:
16 pieces Jumbo pasta shells
4 large eggs
3 lbs. FRESH ricotta cheese
2 lbs diced FRESH mozzarella cheese
1 cup shredded asiago cheese
½ cup fresh parsley
Salt & pepper to taste
¼ cup FRESH chopped basil (optional)

In a hot pan with olive oil, bring heat down to medium,
and sauté the garlic until the garlic turns to <u>very</u> light brown.
Add the onion, and herbs, sauté for 10 minutes.
Put in the tomato paste and slowly stir in until mixed in well.
Slowly add the tomato sauce and crushed tomatoes, simmer
for ½ to 45 minutes.
Meanwhile, bring a large pot of salted water to a boil.
In a mixing bowl combine the ricotta, ½ the asiago cheese,
eggs, parsley, basil (optional), and a dash of salt and pepper,
mix at medium-low setting, until most of the lumps are gone, leave a few.
Fold in the mozzarella cheese.
Add the shells to the boiling water and cook for 12 to 15 minutes,
or until they are softened but still undercooked in the center.
Drain pasta, and cool thoroughly.
Fill shells with rounded teaspoons of the mixture and arrange
 seam side down in a casserole dish.
Top shells with the cool sauce, asiago cheese and place in
a broiler for 10 minutes or until the cheese starts to bubble.
Serve with a simple green salad and a loaf of hard crust garlic bread

Pork

Here are my favorite pork dishes, full of flavor.

Asian Style Barbecued Pork Tenderloin

I received the recipe over the internet from a lady named Susan in the U.K. We were in a recipe chat room. She suggested this recipe for a party my wife and I were hosting in the summer on our backyard deck. It turned to be the conversation of the night, there is a little work involved, but the outcome is something to be proud of.

Marinade:
½ cup soy sauce
2 ½ teaspoons sesame oil
1 ½ teaspoon minced garlic
2 teaspoons fresh lime
2 teaspoons rice wine vinegar
1 ½ teaspoons ground ginger
½ teaspoon sugar
1 (3lbs.) Boneless pork tenderloin

Mix soy sauce, sesame oil, garlic, lime juice, vinegar, ginger, and sugar.
Place the tenderloin in a large zip lock plastic bag and pour the entire marinade in it, seal it and store in the refrigerator for 3 hours.

Asian Style Barbecue Sauce:
¾ prepared Barbecued sauce (I used Sweet Baby Ray's)
2 teaspoons soy sauce
1 tablespoon peanut oil
1 tablespoon rice wine vinegar
½ teaspoons minced garlic
½ teaspoon ground Anise seeds
½ teaspoon ground ginger

Mix entire ingredients in a sauce pan and simmer together for ½ hour.

Prepare a hot barbecue grill over medium hot coals (gas heat).
Place the tenderloin on the grill and turn it occasionally, until it has
reached an internal temperature of 150 – 160 degrees (45 minutes to an hour).
Allow the tenderloin to stand for 15 minutes and slice in ¼ inch slices.
Drizzle the barbecue sauce over the meat slices after it has been arranged on a leaf lettuce lined, and orange sliced dish. Place the remaining sauce in a bowl and serve it at the side of the dish.

Dennis' Bourbon Infused Pork Tenderloin

The only way to enjoy a pork tenderloin. The combination of bourbon and the sweetness of brown sugar succumb a perfect flavor. Choose you vegetable. Be careful, I suggest a dark green vegetable and some type of yam.

¼ cup soy sauce
¼ cup bourbon
2 tablespoons brown sugar
2 cloves garlic, halved
3 pounds pork tenderloin

Mix together soy sauce, bourbon, brown sugar, and garlic. Pour over pork, cover, and refrigerate at least 2 hours, turning occasionally.
Preheat oven to 325 degrees F (165 degrees C). Remove pork from marinade, and place on rack of shallow roasting pan.
Bake for 45 minutes or until meat thermometer registers 160 degrees.

Glazed Honey Pork Chops

My family is not fond of many pork recipes. They will eat pork only if I hide the strong pork flavor. By adding a glaze to the chops, enables the strong pork flavor to hide behind the sweetness. I like to serve them with smashed red ski potatoes and fried green beans.

1 cup fine bread crumbs
½ cup brown sugar
¼ cup Spanish paprika
2 tablespoons buckwheat honey
2 teaspoons garlic powder
2 teaspoons sea salt
2 teaspoons cracked pepper

Mix all ingredients well.

Place pork chop in mixture and press and rub until well coated. Grill to medium, or pan fry with very small amount of cooking oil,

Dennis' Favorite Breaded Pork Steaks

This is a recipe that I and my family enjoy. I began to prepare a basic marinara sauce for my mother and family, since pork is not one of their favorite meats. So I had the sauce as a back up, for a simple pasta dish to satisfy them all. I decided to incorporate the two and came up with this succulent recipe. They know have no complaints on me serving pork steaks for dinner.

4 – 6 lean pork steaks (can be trimmed, leave some fat)
2 cups all purpose flour
½ cup Italian bread crumbs
3 large eggs
1 cup whole milk
2-1 tablespoon Italian seasonings
2-1 tablespoon season salt (regular salt will do also)
2-1 teaspoon black pepper
½ teaspoon nutmeg
1 large thin sliced onion
5 cloves garlic sliced
1 (15 oz.) can stewed tomatoes
1 (15 oz.) can tomato puree`
1 (15 oz.) can plum tomatoes
½ (6 oz.) can tomato paste
2 teaspoons sugar
Olive oil
4 cups cooked Jasmine rice (boil with ¼ cup Paprika for color)

Prepare an egg wash with the eggs and milk.
Combine in a large enough bowl to fit a pork steak, the flour,
bread crumbs, 1 portion of each; Italian seasoning, salt & pepper.
Dunk the pork steak in the wash and then into the breading and
fry to medium over medium heat, in enough olive oil to cover the
steak half way the thickness. Once done set the steaks aside.
Keeping the pan hot, add a little more olive oil to cover the
entire bottom of the pan, toss in the onion and garlic, sauté until just tender.
Add the remaining seasonings and sugar, sauté for 5 minutes.
Add the tomato paste and mix well.
Add in the other tomato products and simmer for 15 minutes.
Completely submerge the pork steaks in the sauce and simmer
very low for 1 hour.
Serve with rice and warm garlic bread

Dennis' Honey Butter Holiday Ham

Why do we have to wait for the holidays? Go ahead, make it anytime.

1 (12 pound) bone-in ham
¾ cup butter, softened
¾ cup honey
½ cup whole cloves (optional)
Preheat the oven to 350 degrees

Cut 1 inch deep criss-crosses into the flat side of the ham. In a small bowl, mix together the butter and honey. Slather onto the ham, making sure to get in the crevices too. Insert cloves into the ham if desired. Place in a roasting pan.
Bake for 4 hours in the preheated oven, or 20 minutes per pound. The internal temperature should reach 160 degrees F (70 degrees C). Baste every 20 minutes with the drippings. Remove, slice, serve, and savor.

Ham with Cherry Sauce

Ham was never this good. The sweet cherries add the final touch to the saltiness. The cherry sauce should be drizzled over the top then served in a bowl on the side for a colorful presentation.

1 (8 pound) fully-cooked, bone-in ham (I like an old-fashion best)
1 cup packed brown sugar
3 tablespoons maple syrup
1 teaspoon ground mustard
½ cup sugar
3 tablespoons cornstarch
1 cup cold water
1 (16.5 ounce) can pitted dark sweet cherries
2 tablespoons lemon juice
1 teaspoon almond extract

Place ham in a roasting pan.
Score surface of ham with shallow diagonal cuts, making diamond shapes. Combine the brown sugar, syrup and mustard; rub over ham and press into cuts. Cover and bake at 325 degrees for 1-3/4 to 2 hours or until a meat thermometer reads 140 degrees.
For cherry sauce, in a saucepan, combine the sugar, cornstarch and water until smooth.
Add cherries and bring to a boil; cook and stir for 2 minutes or until thickened. Remove from the heat; stir in lemon juice and extract. Serve with ham.

Iris' Puerto Rican Gandule Rice

A Puerto Rican dish with local Hawaiian flavor. Labor intensive, but also delicious. One ingredient, pigeon pea, is native to Africa and is also called 'Congo pea' and 'no-eyed pea'; achiote seeds are slightly musky-flavored seeds of the annatto tree, available whole or ground in East Indian, Spanish and Latin American markets. Buy whole seeds when they're a rusty red color; brown seeds are old and flavorless. Achiote seeds are also called 'annatto' which, in its paste and powder form is used in the United States to color butter, margarine, cheese and smoked fish.

1 cup vegetable oil
3 pounds pork shoulder, cubed
3 tablespoons achiote (annatto) seeds
2 cups chopped onion
2 cups chopped fresh cilantro
12 cloves garlic, crushed
2 tablespoons salt
1 teaspoon ground black pepper
2 (8 ounce) cans tomato sauce
1 (15 ounce) can pigeon peas, drained
15 ounces black olives, pitted and halved
8 cups uncooked calrose rice, rinsed
9 cups water

Heat 2 tablespoons of the oil in a large saucepan over medium high heat. Add pork and brown in oil. Meanwhile, place remaining oil in a small saucepan over medium heat and add achiote seeds. Heat until oil becomes very dark orange/red. Remove from heat and set aside.

To the browned pork add the onion, cilantro, garlic, salt and pepper. Cook to reduce veggies, and then add the tomato sauce, pigeon peas and olives. Mix well. Strain achiote/oil mixture into pork mixture and stir together. Reduce heat to low and let simmer for 10 minutes.

Add uncooked rice and water to pork mixture; stir well. Raise temperature to high, cover saucepan and bring all to a boil. Stir again, reduce heat to low and cover; let cook on low about 10 minutes. Remove cover, stir again, replace cover and cook another 10 minutes; stir again. Remove from heat and allow to stand 15 minutes.

Iris' Puerto Rican Pork Roast – Penine

I can't get enough of this. My friend Iris makes this roast during the holidays. I can't wait for a plateful. Sasoon' and Adobo seasonings are combinations of spices created in Puerto Rico. They add an intense flavor like no other

8 cloves garlic, peeled
¼ cup salt
¼ cup black pepper
2 teaspoons chopped fresh oregano
3 tablespoons olive oil
1 (10 pound) pork picnic roast
4 yucca (cassava) roots, peeled and sliced
2 envelopes Sasoon' seasonings (you can find in a Puerto Rican grocery mkt.)
2 Tablespoons Adobo (you can find in a Puerto Rican grocery mkt.)

Preheat the oven to 425 degrees F (220 degrees C).
Place the garlic, salt, pepper, oregano, and olive oil into the container of a food processor or blender and process until smooth.
Use a small knife to make several incisions in the fresh ham.
Insert the garlic paste into each one using a small spoon.
Rub with a generous of sasoon'
Sprinkle with Adobo
Place the ham in a roaster, and cover.
Bake for 1 1/2 hours in the preheated oven, then check every 15 minutes or so, until the internal temperature reaches 175 degrees, when taken with a meat thermometer.
While the meat is roasting, place the yucca in a large pot of boiling water. Cook until fork tender, and drain. Serve with pork roast.

Pasta with Kielbasa, Tomatoes and Bell Peppers

This recipe is fast and easy. It is one of my favorite quick meals. Simple yet bursting with taste from all different flavors. If you are in a hurry, try this recipe, you will not be disappointed.

1 Non-stick oven-proof skillet
1 lb. kielbasa, skinned, cut in ½ to 1" pieces
3 tablespoons oil
1 large onion, finely chopped
1 large tomatoes, plunged into boiling water, skinned, seeds   removed, and diced
1 bell pepper, red or green, finely chopped
8 oz. pasta, bow ties or similar
1½ cup dry red or white wine
Parmesan cheese

Pre-set oven 350 degrees

Cook pasta in boiling water until el dente, cool and set aside in cold water

In skillet sauté onion in oil, at medium heat until soft.
Add kielbasa and cook 4 minutes.
Add tomatoes, pepper, stirring all the while.
Add pasta and continue cooking over low heat for 8 minutes.
Add wine, salt, and pepper to taste.
Stir thoroughly.
Sprinkle with parmesan cheese.
Place skillet in oven for 30 minutes.

I sometimes serve this over a bed of steamed rice.

Pork Chops in Pineapple Sauce

This is an easy way to prepare pork chops, where your guests will think you were sweating in the kitchen all day. The sweet and tangy flavor of the sauce accompanies the chicken very well. Any cut of chicken works well.

Fry pork chops medium rare as you would normally.

Sauce:
¾ cup vinegar
1 cup sugar
2 tablespoon corn starch
1 tablespoon mustard
1 tablespoon Worcestershire
113 oz. can pineapple chunks and juice
1 medium green pepper sliced thick
1 tomato quartered (optional)
2 tablespoons sherry (optional)
1 small can frozen orange juice

Season and fry the pork chops, leaving them medium rare

In saucepan stir vinegar into cornstarch and sugar until it is smooth and cook until clear. Add mustard, Worcestershire sauce, pineapple juice, and frozen orange juice, stirring until well blended, about 12-20 minutes.
Before serving time, add pineapple chunks, pepper tomato and sauce to pork chops and broil until glazed.
Serve with a side of fried rice and a vegetable.

Robin's Apricot Glazed Pork Chops

The apricots add a flavorful aroma to this dish. Great with scalloped potatoes.

1 (15 ounce) can apricot halves, do not drain
4 (3/4 inch thick) bone-in pork loin chops
1 tablespoon butter
1 tablespoon cornstarch
2 tablespoons cold water
salt and pepper to taste

Place apricots in a food processor or blender; cover and process until coarsely chopped.
In a large skillet, brown pork chops in butter over medium-high heat. Add apricots. Bring to a boil.
Reduce heat; cover and simmer for 7-10 minutes or until meat juices run clear. Remove the chops and keep warm.
Combine cornstarch and cold water until smooth; stir into apricot mixture.
Bring to a boil; cook and stir for 1 minute or until thickened.
Season with salt and pepper.
Serve over pork chops.

Sam's Italian Style Country Ribs

My good friend Sam Palise (W.M. F&AM) gave me this recipe. It is a treat to enjoy a country pork rib with an Italian flair. This is a hearty dish and does well in the colder months, but nothing stops me from making it for a party when it is a pot luck affair.

3 – 4 lbs country ribs
1 large chopped onion
5 cloves chopped garlic
1 medium chopped green pepper
½ lb. fresh sliced mushrooms or a 10 oz. can of mushrooms
1 15 oz can tomato puree
½ 6 oz. can tomato paste
2 15 oz. cans tomato sauce
2 tablespoons Italian seasoning
1 Tablespoon salt
½ teaspoon pepper
1 teaspoon sugar
Olive oil
Boiled Pasta

Sauté the country ribs in olive oil, set aside.
In the same hot pan sauté the vegetables tender.
Add the seasonings sauté 5 minutes.
Add the tomato paste and mix well, combine the remaining tomato products simmer 20 minutes.
Submerge the country ribs, in the sauce in a baking dish and bake at 250 degrees for 1 ½ hours.
Serve on top of a bed of spaghetti, or any type of string pasta, with a fresh lettuce salad and hard crust bread.

Smothered Pork Chops

When I began to cook at my deli/soul food carry out in downtown Detroit, I hired my good friend Loraine she explained to me that if you want to cook good soul food, "ya gotta put grandma's toe in it" I remember her standing next to me until she was satisfied of the result of her old family recipes. Lorraine was born and raised in Mississippi, and this recipe is as southern as it can get.

6 Lean thick center cut bone-in pork chops
2 large beaten eggs
2-1 cup milk portions
2 large thin sliced onions
3 cloves chopped garlic
3 cups all purpose flour
1 teaspoon garlic powder
1 teaspoon sugar
2 teaspoons paprika
1 tablespoon seasoning salt
1 teaspoon pepper
1-2 cups canola oil

Prepare an egg wash with the milk and eggs
Combine all the dry ingredients in a bowl, mix well
Dip the chops in egg wash, then placing in the breading and fry until medium rare, save the remaining breading for later.
Once all finished frying, add the onions and garlic until tender, yet still firm.
Remove as much onion and garlic as possible and set aside.
Cool the oil down to room temperature and add the milk and flour used for breading, stirring slowly to remove any lumps.
Bring to a simmer; keep adding flour, slowly stirring, until loose gravy has been formed.
Place ½ the gravy in a baking dish, add the chops then the onions and topping it off with the remaining gravy. (Make sure the chops are completely submerged in the gravy)
Bake at 300 degrees for 45 minutes.
Serve with white rice and a green vegetable.

Poultry

Poultry has become prevalent on dinner tables throughout the world. As poultry becomes frequently more popular, countless recipes are being created everyday

Chicken Ooh-La-La

Another fast and easy dish where your guests will think you have been in the kitchen all day. A nice low-cost way to empress your guests a poultry dish.

¾ cup Italian seasoned fine dry bread crumbs
¼ cup grated parmesan cheese
6 whole large boneless, skinless chicken breast, skinned, split
½ cup sliced green onion
2 tablespoons butter or margarine
2 tablespoons all purpose flour
1 cup whole milk
1 10 oz. package frozen chopped spinach, thawed and well drained
1 4 oz. package boiled ham slices diced

Combine bread crumbs and cheese; dip chicken breast halves in crumb mixture to coat lightly.
Arrange in a 9 x 13 baking dish.
Set remaining crumb mixture aside.
In saucepan cook onion in butter or margarine till tender.
Blend in flour; stir in milk.
Cook and stir till thickened and bubbly.
Cook and stir 1 minute more.
Stir in spinach and ham.
Spoon spinach mixture over chicken; sprinkle with remaining crumb mixture.
Bake uncovered in 350 degrees oven for 40 to 45 minutes or till done.

Makes 12 servings.

Chicken with Pineapple Sauce

This is an easy way to prepare chicken. The sweet and tangy flavor of the sauce accompanies the chicken perfectly. Any cut of chicken works well.

Bake chicken breast or cut up fryers as you would normally.

Sauce:
¾ cup vinegar
1 cup sugar
2 tablespoon corn starch
1 tablespoon mustard
1 tablespoon Worcestershire
113 oz. can pineapple chunks and juice
1 medium green pepper sliced thick
1 tomato quartered (optional)
2 tablespoons sherry (optional)
1 small can frozen orange juice

Prepare sauce while chicken is baking.

In saucepan stir vinegar into cornstarch and sugar until it is smooth and cook until clear. Add mustard, Worcestershire sauce, pineapple juice, and frozen orange juice, stirring until well blended, about 12-20 minutes.
Before serving time, add pineapple chunks, pepper tomato and sauce to chicken and broil until glazed.
Serve with a side of steamed white rice and a dark green vegetable such as steamed broccoli.

Cornish Game Hens with Wild Rice Stuffing

Over the years, I realized that there will be guests that never had Cornish game hens. Cornish hens are all dark meat, which may cause a few of your guests that prefer white meat to be hesitant. I always stuffed the hens, producing a nice presentation, on which your guest to be more courageous and try one.

6 tablespoons unsalted butter, divided
¼ cup finely chopped onion
2 tablespoons finely chopped celery
1 teaspoon finely chopped fresh thyme leaves
1½ cups cooked wild rice
1 tablespoon minced flat-leaf parsley, plus sprigs for garnish
1/3 cup toasted pecan pieces, broken
2 tablespoons dried cranberries
2 tablespoons dried currants
4 dried apricots, diced
Kosher salt and freshly ground black pepper
4 Cornish hens, patted dry
1 tablespoon balsamic vinegar

In a medium skillet, heat 2 tablespoons of the butter over medium-low heat. Sauté the onions and celery until softened, about 10 minutes.
Add the thyme and cook for 1 minute more. In a mixing bowl combine the onion mixture with the rice, parsley, nuts and dried fruits and season with salt and pepper to taste.
Place 1/2 cup of the stuffing into the cavity of each hen.
Tie the legs of each bird together with kitchen twine.

Preheat the oven to 400 degrees.

Melt the remaining butter with the vinegar. Brush the birds all over with the butter mixture and season with salt and pepper.
Put the hens on a rack in a large roasting pan, breast-side up.
Roast the hens until an instant read thermometer inserted in the thigh registers 170 degrees for about 80 minutes.
Set the birds aside at room temperature, loosely covered with foil, for 10 minutes before carving.
Split hens in half through the breast with a sharp knife or poultry shears, and keep the stuffing intact.
Arrange bird's skin-side up, on a platter, garnish with sprigs of parsley and serve.

Dennis' Chicken Rice Bake

This is a recipe I invented by adding what I thought went well together. It is a combination as I can see a chicken casserole, and chicken Creole.

2 – 3 lbs. cut up chicken legs and thighs
1 large sliced onion
2 sliced celery stalks
1 chopped green bell pepper
4 cloves chopped garlic
1 can chopped, or stewed tomatoes
1 can okra (optional)
1 table spoon tomato paste
2 tablespoons white sugar
2 tablespoons Creole seasonings
1 teaspoon sea salt
1 teaspoon black pepper
2 cups par boiled white rice boiled in chicken stock reserving the liquid
Canola oil

Salt and pepper the chicken pieces, fry in oil with the garlic
until ¾ done (medium).
Add the onions, green pepper, and celery.
Add the tomato sauce, okra, (optional) tomato paste, Creole
seasonings and sugar.
In a baking dish place the rice at the bottom, lightly salt and pepper,
carefully, place the chicken only on top of the rice allowing the
rice to remain completely on the bottom.
Top with the vegetables.
Mix together, the remaining sauce and enough chicken stock liquid
to allow the rice to be submerged.
Cover and bake until the rice has absorbed all the liquid.
Note: It is better not to add enough liquid and add more as you need,
than to add too much liquid with the result of the rice being mushy.

Dennis' Chicken Livers and White Rice

I made this dish in the spur of the moment. A very flavorful soul food dish, if you like chicken livers. The dish sits in a bed of white rice that produces its own gravy. Scrumptious with creamed sweet corn!

2 lbs. chicken livers
1 large onion thin sliced
4 cloves garlic thin sliced
1½ cups all purpose flour
2 teaspoons Cajun seasoning (I use Emeril's Bayou magic)
2 teaspoons seasoning salt
1 teaspoon fresh cracked pepper
2 tablespoons dried parsley flakes
2 cubes chicken bouillon
2 cups white rice
water
vegetable oil

In a medium saucepan add the rice, parsley flakes, chicken bouillon, and 4 ½ cups water.
Boil until done and set aside.

In a frying pan add oil until the pan has around ¼ inch on the bottom and set on the stove over medium-high heat. Careful not to allow to smoke.
Add the onions and garlic until clarified.
In a bowl add all the dry ingredients, toss the livers in it and fry with the onions and garlic for 15 minutes, reserving the extra dry mixture.
Pour in to start 2 cups of water, carefully stir not to disturb the livers. If the gravy is too thick add a little more water. If it is too loose, add a little more flour.
Once nice gravy has been determined, simmer for 20 minutes and serve over a bed of whit rice.

Dennis' Chicken Marsala

I never gave this dish a second thought; it never did anything for me until I perfected this recipe. It is a rendition of a restaurant that my wife and I visit often.

4 – 6 boneless, skinless chicken breasts
Spices/herbs to sprinkle over:
Granulated garlic
Onion powder
Italian seasoning
Sea salt
Black pepper
Paprika
Olive oil

For sauce:
1/3 cup butter
2 slices prosciutto diced
2 teaspoons shallots minced
2 teaspoons garlic minced
2 (4 oz.) cans sliced mushrooms drained
½ cup Marsala wine
¼ teaspoon ground black pepper
1 cup chicken stock
2 teaspoons corn starch
1 teaspoon fresh minced parsley
2 tablespoons heavy cream

Sprinkle the herbs and spiced over the chicken breasts and sauté the in olive oil, set aside.

Melt butter over low heat in a sauce pan, turn up to medium heat and sauté the prosciutto, add shallots and garlic sauté for 2 minutes.
Add Marsala wine, simmer for 1 minute then add the mushrooms and black pepper simmer over low heat for 5 minutes.
Dissolve the corn starch in the chicken stock and add to the sauce pan and simmer until the sauce begins to thicken.
Mix in the cream and parsley slow simmer for 15 minutes.
Add the chicken to the sauce and bake for 25 minutes in a 350 degree oven.
Serve over a bed of angel hair pasta, top with parmesan cheese, and a hard crust bread.

Dennis' Grilled Marinated Chicken Breasts

This is another one of the family's favorites. The girls like the chicken served with my super smashed potatoes and asparagus spears. I always make enough so that there are leftovers for tomorrow's lunch. This can be done on an electric grill indoors.

For marinate:
¾ cup extra virgin olive oil
Juice of 3 lemons
2 tablespoons paprika
2 table spoons dried chopped chives
2 tablespoons honey
1 tablespoons seasoned salt
2 teaspoons brown sugar
2 teaspoons granulated garlic
2 teaspoons oregano
½ teaspoon cayenne pepper
Mix together well, if more liquid is needed to for a loose paste, add small amounts of vegetable oil.

6 Chicken breasts

Split the breasts in half, marinate for 24 hours.
Grill over med/high flame until done turning twice per side.

Turducken - A Cajun Thanksgiving Dinner

This is very difficult to make. I have seen these already prepared bird(s) sold on the internet. I can't tell how well or what quality they are. I once tried it, but had the local butcher debone the birds for me. Believe me, it was well worth the money to save all that time and effort

20 - 25 lb. turkey
4 - 5 lb. duck
1½ lb. chicken
Oyster dressing (see recipe)
Corn bread dressing (see recipe)
Dirty rice dressing (see recipe)
Chicken stock (I used a few large cans)

Turn fowl over onto breast.
Start with a small sharp paring knife or any small knife with a sharp blade.
Using tip of knife, follow along backbone to cut the skin.
Start at top, using tip of knife to loosen skin, being careful not to break the skin by keeping tip of knife against the bone at all times.
When the fleshy parts are reached, continue to remove in same manner by keeping the point of knife blade against bone structure and moving in very small strokes to cut fleshy parts away from bone and leaving it attached to the skin.

When the thigh is reached, take point of knife and go completely around thigh bone removing flesh.
Using blade of knife, scrape bone until completely free of flesh and continue to expose bone from flesh by pulling and scraping with knife blade until joint of thigh bone and drumstick is reached.
Then again using point of knife, go around the joint to release any flesh attendance.
When the joint is cleared of flesh, continue to pull out and scrape bone until the end of drumstick is reached.
Use the same procedure on the wing.
The point of the breast is going to be the next challenge because the skin and bone are separated only by a small amount of fat and must be approached with the of the knife very slowly making small cuts until skin is removed from center of breast bone.
Once both sides are done and carcass is completely removed, lay skin and mean on a flat surface. Season inside generously. Fill with 1/4" layer of oyster dressing.
Use same boning procedure on duck. When all bones and carcass are removed, lay on flat surface on top of turkey and fill with 1/4" corn bread dressing.
Next, use same boning procedure for chicken. When all bones and carcass are removed, lay on flat surface on top of duck and fill with 1/4" dirt rice dressing.
Sew up each fowl separately, stating with the chicken, then duck. Then sew all together with the turkey. Cover with foil.
Cook at 275 degrees for 8 hours.

Chicken Cordon Bleu – Lionel Gemus
Poi trine de pullet Madera - (Chicken breast/Madeira sauce)

I prefer this recipe for Cordon Bleu over any recipe out there. My friend mike tells me his father has perfected this dish after long hours in his kitchen experimenting with different flavors. A true French Canadian entrée. The sauce is made up of Madeira wine, giving a sweet flavor throughout. I like to serve this with simple boiled red skin potatoes adding a touch of the wine sauce over top.

6 Supremes of chicken breasts
6 slices of baked ham
4 oz. grated Swiss cheese
   Sea salt and pepper
   Madeira wine
1½ oz cognac
½ cup heavy cream
1 cup brown sauce
1 stick clarified butter

Flatten breasts between sheets of wax paper on hard surface with wood mallet.
Season with salt and pepper.
Place ham slices over breasts.
Cover generously with grated Swiss cheese.
Pour a few drops of Madeira wine over cheese.
Roll breasts, tucking in the sides, and set aside.
Clarify butter in large skillet.
Sautee rolled breasts on all sides, including ends by turning with tongs.
Remove meat and store in warm oven.
Pour out most of remaining butter from skillet.
 Replace with 1 ½ oz cognac, scraping bottom to pick up all remaining bits.
Turn heat to high temperature, ignite and flame.
Pour in 2 oz. Madeira wine, 1 cup brown sauce, ½ cup cream.
Lower fire to moderate high heat and continue to stir all ingredients until the bubble and have the consistency of syrup.
Roll chicken breasts in sauce and place them in serving dish.
Add more sauce over each breast.
Any additional sauce can be served on the side.
Decorate with you preferred garnish.

Lorraine's Low fat 20-minute Chicken Creole

Lorraine is an icon when it came to teach me all about southern soul food. Everything she prepared, had love in it. She would stand in the kitchen, singing and smiling. I will never forget her expertise, patience and sheer love for the art of cooking. I don't have to explain any opinion of whether I like the recipe or not, if it begins with her name, it is guaranteed scrumptious.

4 medium chicken breast halves (1 ½ lbs. total),
    skinned, boned and cut into 1 inch strips
1 (14 oz.) can stewed tomatoes, chopped up
1 cup (low sodium) chili sauce
1½ cups chopped green paper (1 large)
½ cup chopped celery
¼ cup chopped onion
3 cloves garlic, minced
1 tablespoon chopped fresh basil or 1 teaspoon dried
1 teaspoon dried parsley
¼ teaspoons dried red pepper
½ teaspoon sea salt
Nonstick spray coating

Spray deep skillet with nonstick cooking spray, and preheat pan over high heat.
Cook chicken strips in hot skillet, while stirring every 3 – 5 minutes or until no longer pink.
Reduce heat, Add entire ingredients and simmer for 20 – 30 minutes.
Serve over brown rice or whole wheat pasta.

POULET (CHICKEN) BLANC – Lionel Gemus

A real traditional French Canadian chicken dish. It has all the flavors, hot, tangy, and sweet. I enjoy serving this for friends who haven't a clue of what French food is about. Simple enough so that your guests will not hesitate to attempt the first bite.

3 chicken breast (6 half breast) deboned
3 tablespoons olive oil
3 cloves garlic, finely chopped
2 tablespoons lemon juice
¼ teaspoon thyme
½ teaspoon salt
1 stick butter
4 shallots, finely chopped
5 tablespoons flour
3 cups whole milk
Dash black pepper (to taste)
2 dashes Tabasco
Pinch ground nutmeg

Placed the deboned between two pieces of wax paper and with the flat of your cleaver, pound the meat hard until it spreads almost double. Slice the flattened breasts into strips. Marinate for one hour in the olive oil, garlic, lemon juice, thyme, and salt. Stir a few times.

After the meat has been marinated, melt the butter in your heavy skillet, add the oil, and fry the strips of chicken for 2 minutes on each side. (Do not overcook).
Remove the chicken and add the shallots to the pan; Sautee until tender.
Add the flour (lower heat considerably when cooking flour), mix well and stirring constantly, cook 4 minutes.
Raise the heat a bit, add the milk slowly, stirring all the while and mixing well. Salt and pepper to taste, then add the two dashes of Tabasco.
When the milk begins to simmer, return the chicken to the pan and allow to simmer slowly for a few minutes until the sauce is thickened.
Add the nutmeg, stir, and the dish is ready to serve.
Serve over noodles or a slice of toast. Serves four to six, hopefully.

Stirring all the while and mixing well.

Robin's Chicken Paprikash

This recipe is barely any more complicated than chopping provisions up and boiling them in a pot. If I use store-bought spaetzel, (it is ok, but NOT homemade). I can make a complete pot of paprikash and have all the dishes cleaned in 45 minutes.

4 lbs. chicken (Robin uses boneless. Skinless breasts, I prefer legs and thighs, they tend
   to be more flavorful)
2-24 oz. sour cream
2-48 oz. chicken broth
2 onion
¼ cup Hungarian paprika
5 cloves chopped garlic
2 tablespoon sea salt
2 teaspoon ginger
3 bay leaves
corn starch or flour

Make spaetzel; put in a bowl. Alternately, you can buy spaetzel from the store, or prepare any type of noodles you prefer. Spaetzel is authentic.
This seems to be a heretical recipe, because almost everyone I speak to, claims that the batter/dough should require cutting with a knife. I'll let this recipe speak for itself.

1 cups milk
3 cups flour (use a high gluten)
6 large eggs
3 teaspoons dried parsley flakes

Get a pot of water going at a high boil.
Mix the milk, flour, parley, and eggs in a bowl. The resulting batter should be a little thicker than cake mix: a tiny bit stiff, but definitely not "dough".
With a spoon, drop small blobs of batter into the boiling water, and let boil for about 20 minutes. Then you may fish out the spaetzel.

Cut up the chicken breasts into small pieces or the leave the chicken legs and thighs whole and fry until medium (still with a little blood in the middle). Leave everything in the pan and set the pan aside for a moment.
Chop up the onion into small pieces.
Put the chicken, onions, and chicken broth into a pot. For now, use just enough broth to keep everything submerged, but don't flood it. You should have some broth left over (maybe around 16 ounces); the remaining broth will be used below.

(Continued)

Stir in the spices (paprika, garlic, salt, ginger, bay leaves).
Simmer to let the chicken and onions cook thoroughly.
When the chicken and onions are fully cooked, add corn starch or flour as a thickening agent, by mixing it into the remaining broth and pouring it into the pot. (If you're out of broth, use water; but ideally you will have exactly enough broth for this.) Remove from heat and let it thicken.
Finally, add the sour cream, and it's ready to serve over spaetzel.

Be advised that you need to keep the water at a high boil for this to work: the surfaces of the blobs really need to cook as soon as they hit the water. Then they magically don't stick together.
Also the blobs will expand as they cook, so try not to make them very large. One way or another, you'll probably have to chop them up with a spatula when you're done anyway.

Poulet (Chicken) Blanc

A delicate dish that allows the pasta to accompany the flavors from the sauce. I serve this meal with a spinach green salad, steamed cauliflower and garlic bread, making this meal light enough to end with a more heavy dessert.

3 chicken breast (6 half breast) deboned
3 tablespoons olive oil
3 cloves garlic, finely chopped
2 tablespoons lemon juice
¼ teaspoon thyme
½ teaspoon salt
1 stick butter
4 shallots, finely chopped
5 tablespoons flour
3 cups whole milk
Dash black pepper (to taste)
2 dashes Tabasco
Pinch ground nutmeg

Placed the deboned between two pieces of wax paper and with the flat of your cleaver, pound the meat hard until it spreads almost double.

Slice the flattened breasts into strips and marinate for one hour in the olive oil, garlic, lemon juice, thyme, and salt. Stir a few times.

After the meat has been marinated, melt the butter in your heavy skillet, add the oil, and fry the strips of chicken for 2 minutes on each side. (Do not overcook too long).

Remove the chicken and add the shallots to the pan; Sautee until tender, adding the flour (lower heat considerably when cooking flour), mix well and stirring constantly, cook 4 minutes.

Raise the heat a bit, add the milk slowly, stirring all the while and mixing well.

Salt and pepper to taste, and then add the two dashes of Tabasco.

When the milk begins to simmer, return the chicken to the pan and allow to simmer slowly for a few minutes until the sauce is thickened and the chicken is heated.

Add the nutmeg, stir, and the dish is ready to serve.

Serve over noodles.

Serves four to six, hopefully.

.

Seafood

With all the concern of a heart smart diet, seafood has been consumed more frequent than ever before. Being raised with Mediterranean heritage, seafood was on our table twice a week.

Manuel's Calamari or Octopus Stew
Stuffat Tal-Klamari (Squid) or Stuffat Tal Qarnita (Octopus)

This is probably my father's favorite seafood dish. He didn't prepare it often because of the time and effort evolved. This dish should be taken under consideration; one must have at least 3 – 4 hours of free time. When served, you will realize how much this meal was worth the time put into it. Serve over a dish of hot spaghetti, and top with fresh parmesan cheese.

1 large peeled onion
4 cloves chopped garlic
2 to 3 pounds cleaned, fresh octopus or calamari cut into 1 inch pieces
1 large can crushed tomatoes
2 tablespoons tomato paste
1 teaspoon each oregano, basil, mint leafs, and bay leafs
¼ cup small capers
½ cup sliced black olives
¼ cup extra virgin olive oil
3 cups water
1 teaspoon sea salt
2 teaspoon freshly ground pepper
1 cup red wine
Parmesan cheese

Boil Spaghetti in salted water
Once done, set aside in cool water

In a large frying pan, sauté' the onion and garlic in olive oil until translucent.
Add octopus or calamari, sauté for ½ hour on medium heat not allowing the mixture to dry, if so add more olive oil.
Add wine and bay leaf.
Add remaining ingredients except for cheese, and simmer at low heat
for approx. 1 ½ hours.

Dennis' Glazed Salmon

After returning home from a hectic day at work, this dish can be easily prepared without losing any flavor. The glaze can be made days before and placed in a jar for up to 2 weeks. This glaze adds a sweet yet tart flavor to your fish, allowing the delicate flavor of salmon still come through. A side of white rice and a green leafy vegetable works well.

½ cup brown sugar
½ cup whipped butter or margarine
3 tablespoons sesame oil
2 tablespoons buckwheat honey
1 teaspoon garlic powder
1 tablespoon Dijon mustard
1 teaspoon dried dill weed
1 teaspoon hot sauce
1 teaspoon lime juice
2 teaspoon sea salt
1 teaspoon fresh cracked pepper

Blend all ingredients well, spoon on salmon grill skin side down.
DO NOT flip fish. Grill until medium.

Fish with Caper Sauce   (Hut Biz-Zalza Tal-Kappar)

My father was in the kitchen preparing this delicacy, My friend Tony and I were visiting my parents. Tony kept questioned my father why anyone would put cool sauce on fried fish? Without an answer my father asked him to sit down to dinner with us. He was floored, tasting the delicate flavor of fried fish and having the pungent vegetables explode on his palette was something he never forgot. From that day father always made sure to invite Tony over when he prepared this meal. Don't hesitate, try this recipe.

Sauce:
2 large chopped onions
5 cloves finely chopped garlic
1 large can stewed or crushed tomatoes
2 bell sliced peppers (I like to use different colors)
1 cup pitted black olives sliced thin
¼ cup extra virgin olive oil
¼ cup small capers
3 tablespoons tomato paste
2 teaspoons freshly ground pepper
2 cups chicken stock
Few sprigs of each:
   Oregano, basil, parsley and mint
If not available, dried may be used at 1 teaspoon each

Sautee the onions, garlic and peppers until just tender but still firm.
Add the remaining ingredients and simmer for 25 – 30 minutes on
very low heat.
If necessary, add water to the pot to hold a small amount of broth .

 Fish:
4 lbs. fresh boneless fish (Dad used catfish, I like to use a lighter fish like grouper or snapper, any may be used)
2 cups all purpose flour
1 cup either panko or regular bread crumbs
2 tablespoons garlic powder
2 teaspoons each salt and pepper

Mix all dry ingredients in a mixing bowl.
Dust fish and fry in canola oil until crisp.

Let both the fish and sauce set to just above room temperature.
Serve the fish and top with the sauce right when served.
A side of white rice topped with the sauce goes well.

Barbeque Shrimp- Lionel Gemus

This is not barbequed! Because of the preparation, this recipe allows you to enjoy no matter what the weather is outside. Use shrimps with head and all their clothes on. Wash carefully. Spread in a single layer on thick newspapers and let dry thoroughly for an hour.

Heat oven to 350 degrees. In a large shallow roasting pan, spread shrimp evenly. For every pound, use a stick of butter, plus 1 or 2 more sticks for the pan. Spread a layer of fresh black pepper about 1/16" thick all over the shrimp. lay sticks of butter across the peppered shrimp and bake them from 25-45 minute, depending on the amount of shrimp used. Every 10 or 15 minutes take the pan out and turn the shrimp over. Watch them carefully. As soon as they are done, take them out because if they are overcooked, it is almost impossible to remove the skins.

Seasoning Mix:
1 tsp. ground red pepper (preferably cayenne)
1 tsp. black pepper
½ tsp. salt
½ tsp. crushed red pepper
½ tsp. dried thyme leaves
½ tsp. dried rosemary leaves crushed
1/8 tsp dried oregano leaves
1 stick plus 5 tbsp unsalted butter
1 ½ tsp minced garlic
1 tsp Worcestershire sauce
½ cup basic shrimp stock
¼ cup beer at room temperature

Rinse shrimp in cold water.
Combine seasoning mix ingredients in small bowl. Combine 1 stick of butter, the garlic, Worcestershire and seasoning mix in a large skillet over high heat. When the butter is melted, add the shrimp. Cook for 2 minutes, shaking the pan, versus stirring, in a back and forth motion. Add the remaining 5 tbsp butter and the stock; cook and shake pan for 2 minutes. Add the beer and cook and shake the pan 1 minute longer. Remove from heat.
Serve immediately in bowls with lots of French bread on the side, or on a platter with the cooked rice mounded in the middle and the shrimp and sauce surrounding it.
He says a certain percentage of oil is released when butter is melted; shaking the pan in a back and forth motion and the addition of stock to the butter keep the sauce from separating and having an oily texture—stirring doesn't produce the same effect.
Serve with crusty French bread and drawn butter.

Okra Seafood Gumbo - Lionel Gemus

Enjoying a dish makes one think they are in New Orleans. Lionel Gemus moved to New Orleans for 11 years. He renovated his garage into an armature's commercial kitchen. Lionel would stay in there perfecting recipes all day long, at the end of the day; there would be a gathering of friends and family savoring over the new recipes

8 large or 12 small crabs; remove inedible parts (hard shell, feelers, etc).
¾ cup oil
2 lb. okra, cut
1 ½ cups chopped onion
¾ cup chopped celery
½ cup flour
2 quarts hot water
¼ cup oil
¾ lb. peeled and devained shrimp
2 teaspoons salt
½ teaspoon pepper
¾ cups bell pepper

Heat oil. Add okra and tomatoes. Fry until okra is no longer sticky or slimy (about 30 minutes-and this is important). Make a dark brown roux* by cooking flour hot oil. Add onions, celery and bell pepper. Fry 10 minutes. Place roux, okra, hot water, salt and pepper in a large saucepan. Bring to boil. Add crabs and simmer 30 minutes. Add shrimp. Continue cooking 15 minutes. Adjust seasoning. Serve over boiled rice. Makes 6 two cup servings, or 12 one cup servings.

*see separate recipe.

Maria's Spanish Sizzled Citrus Shrimp

This is an authentic Spanish recipe. It came from a friend of mine's mother that lived in Spain most of her life. Fresh flavor that explodes in you mouth. Simply the best.

3 tablespoons lemon juice
3 tablespoons dry white wine
2 teaspoons extra-virgin olive oil
3 cloves garlic
1 pound medium shrimp
1 teaspoon extra-virgin olive oil
1 bay leaf
¼ teaspoon crushed red pepper
¼ teaspoon salt
2 tablespoons chopped fresh parsley

Combine lemon juice, wine, 2 teaspoons oil and garlic in a medium bowl.
Add shrimp and toss to coat.
Cover and marinate in the refrigerator for 15 minutes, tossing occasionally.
Drain well, reserving marinade.
Heat 1 teaspoon oil in a large nonstick skillet over medium-high heat.
Add shrimp and cook, turning once, until barely pink, about 30 seconds per side; transfer to a plate.
Add bay leaf, crushed red pepper and the reserved marinade to the pan; simmer for 4 minutes.
Return the shrimp and any accumulated juices to the pan; heat through.
Season with salt, sprinkle with parsley and serve immediately.

Maria's Seafood Couscous Paella

Another one of my friends mother creations. This is Spanish food at its best. Saffron adds a flavor that no other herb can imitate. The combination of seafood is perfect accompanied with the herbs.

2 teaspoons extra-virgin olive oil
1 medium onion
1 clove garlic
½ teaspoon dried thyme
½ teaspoon fennel seed
¼ teaspoon salt
¼ teaspoon freshly ground pepper
   Pinch of crumbled saffron threads
1 cup no-salt-added diced tomatoes, with juice
¼ cup vegetable broth
4 ounces bay scallops
4 ounces small shrimp
½ cup whole-wheat couscous

Heat oil in a large saucepan over medium heat.
Add onion; cook, stirring constantly, for 3 minutes.
Add garlic, thyme, fennel seed, salt, pepper and saffron; cook for 20 seconds.
Stir in tomatoes, broth and green beans.
Bring to a simmer. Cover, reduce heat and simmer for 2 minutes.
Increase heat to medium, stir in scallops and cook, stirring occasionally, for 2 minutes.
Add shrimp and cook, stirring occasionally, for 2 minutes more.
Stir in couscous, cover, remove from heat and let stand for 5 minutes; fluff.

Maria's Spanish Seafood Stew

I head on down to my favorite seafood market for the freshest ingredients. Using frozen fish is ok but I would wait until I can purchase fresh seafood.

3 tablespoons extra-virgin olive oil
2 medium onions
4 clove chopped garlic
1 teaspoon dried thyme
1 teaspoon fennel seed
½ teaspoon salt
½ teaspoon freshly ground pepper
Pinch of crumbled saffron threads
2 cup no-salt-added diced tomatoes, with juice
½ cup vegetable broth
8 ounces green beans
8 ounces bay scallops
8 ounces small shrimp

Heat oil in a large saucepan over medium heat. Add onion; cook, stirring constantly, for 3 minutes.
Add garlic, thyme, fennel seed, salt, pepper and saffron; cook for 20 seconds.
Stir in tomatoes, broth and green beans.
Bring to a simmer. Cover, reduce heat and simmer for 2 minutes.
Increase heat to medium, stir in scallops and cook, stirring occasionally, for 2 minutes.
Add shrimp and cook, stirring occasionally, for 2 minutes more.
Serves 4

Okra Seafood Gumbo

This is another fast and easy recipe that would have very little effort after a long day at work. Using a crock pot is not out of the question.

¾ cup oil
2 lb. okra, cut
1 ½ cups chopped onion
¾ cup chopped celery
½ cup flour
2 quarts hot water
¼ cup oil
¾ lb. peeled, deveined shrimp
8 large or 12 small crabs; remove inedible parts (hard shell, feelers, etc).
2 teaspoons salt
½ teaspoon pepper
¾ cups bell pepper

Heat oil. Add okra and tomatoes. Fry until okra is no longer sticky or slimy (about 30 minutes-and this is important). Make a dark brown roux* by cooking flour hot oil. Add onions, celery and bell pepper. Fry 10 minutes. Place roux, okra, hot water, salt and pepper in a large saucepan. Bring to boil. Add crabs and simmer 30 minutes. Add shrimp. Continue cooking 15 minutes. Adjust seasoning. Serve over boiled rice. Makes 6 two cup servings, or 12 one cup servings.

*see separate recipe.

Shrimp A La Provencal - Lionel Gemus

4 tbsp olive oil
4 tbsp butter
12 mushrooms, finely chopped
4 cloves garlic, finely chopped
4 tomatoes, seeded
2 teaspoons salt
½ teaspoon pepper
1 ½ -2 teaspoons oregano
1 ½ -2 teaspoons thyme
  Pinch cayenne pepper
2 lbs. shrimp, cleaned with tails left on
4 tablespoons cognac, warmed
1-1 1/3 cups dry white wine
3 or 4 egg yolks
¾ -1 cup chopped parsley
2 cloves garlic, finely chopped

Heat 2 tbsp olive oil and 2 tbsp butter, and add next 8 ingredients.
Cook over medium-high heat for about 15 minutes.
Add cayenne, taste for seasoning and set aside.
Heat remaining olive oil and butter, add shrimp, and cook over medium-high heat 1-2 minutes until shrimp are curled and shells are pink.
Add cognac, flame and add wine.
Add the tomato/mushroom mixture.
Continue to cook about 6 minutes.
Beat a little hot sauce into egg yolks gradually, and then add mixture to sauce. Place shrimp and sauce in shallow dish and sprinkle with chopped garlic and parsley. Serve over rice.

Makes 8 servings.

Trout Amandine – Lionel Gemus

A dish that has been around for a long time. I remember while working at the Detroit Athletic Club, preparing the fish ahead of time so that all we had to do was place them in the broiler. Trout made this is still enjoyed throughout the world.

6 trout fillets
Milk (enough to soak the fillets)
1 ½ salt and pepper to taste
   flour
1 ½ sticks butter, plus 2 tablespoons
4 tablespoons oil
¾ cup slivered almonds
1 teaspoon Worchester sauce
2 drops Tabasco
2 tablespoons lemon juice
2 tablespoons minced parsley

After the fish are filleted, soak them in milk for about ½ hour. Remove from the milk, dry well, and rub with a little salt and pepper. Dust lightly (and I mean lightly) In flour.

Heat a heavy skillet. When it is hot, melt 2 tablespoons of butter and add 4 tablespoons oil. When this is hot, Sautee the trout, browning lightly on each side. Don't over cook. (Most cooks have a tendency to overcook fish, and this destroys both the texture and the flavor. A good rule of thumb would be no more than 2 minutes for each side, slightly more if the fillets are unusually thick.)

When the fish are lightly browned, remove to a platter. (be sure this platter has been warmed. This will prevent the fish from getting soggy.)

Pour out the oil and butter in the pan and add 1 ½ sticks butter. Melt this over low heat and then add the slivered almonds. Cook slowly until the almonds are slightly brown, and then add 1 teaspoon Worcestershire sauce, 2 drops of Tabasco sauce, and 2 tablespoons lemon juice. Mix well and pour over the fillets.

Garnish with 2 tablespoons of minced parsley. This should serve six, with Brabant potatoes is a feast.

Vegetarian

I did this for two years. Great way to live, but It was to difficult more me to continue as my family were always meat lovers

Carmen's Spaghetti with Ricotta
(Agien Bil-Irkotta U Zalza Tal Tadam)

I've known Carmen for a long time. We would hang around the kitchen, drumming up new recipes. This recipe is one that her Mother would prepare while living in Malta. I hesitated at first, wondering if it hadn't enough ingredients. From the first fork full I enjoyed this light, meal.

1 small minced onion
3 cloves peeled, sliced garlic
1 can crushed tomatoes
1 can tomato sauce
2 tablespoons tomato paste
1 tablespoon sugar
1½ lbs. fresh ricotta cheese
¼ cup parmesan cheese
¼ cup olive oil
2 teaspoons salt
2 teaspoons pepper
2 lbs. cooked angel hair pasta

Fry garlic in olive, remove and discard.
Add onion and herbs, sauté until clear.
Add in all tomato ingredients, sugar and bring
down heat to low, simmer 30 minutes.
In a separate bowl, whip eggs and ricotta together
Turn off heat and stir in ricotta cheese
Pour over pasta and top with Parmesan cheese

Ravioli (Ravjul)

There is no difference between Italian and Maltese ravioli. The time and effort are well worth it. I have used the traditional Maltese tomato sauce, but a cream sauce such as Alfredo works well too. Experiment!

Pastry:
2 cups of flour
1 cup semolina or 1 egg slightly beaten
dash of salt
water as necessary to bind dough. let stand to room temperature

Filling:
1 lb. ricotta cheese
2 eggs
1 tablespoon finely chopped Parsley
1 tablespoon grated parmesan cheese
   dash of salt

To make the pastry, mix flour, semolina or egg and salt. Add water
and work into a smooth dough. Rest the dough for one hour.

To make the filling, put all of the ingredients into a bowl. Mix.
Divide Pastry into four pieces and roll into long strips about for inches wide. Dampen the edges with water. Put about one tablespoon of filling ¾ of and inch from the edge of the pastry and 1-1/2 inches apart. Turn one edge of pastry on the other one and press to seal.

Using a ravioli cutter, cut the pastry ½ inch away from filling. Set aside on a floured surface about 10 minuets. Boil in salt water in a large pot. In bottom of the pot place saucer upside down. This will prevent the Ravioli from sticking to bottom of pot.

Serve with spaghetti sauce* and grated cheese.

*See basic Maltese traditional tomato sauce.

Ricotta Torta

Fast, and easy best describes this. Ricotta cheese Torta is basically a quiche' like pie, filled ricotta cheese, covered with a piecrust. This is a very common Sunday morning brunch item. It also makes a wonderful meal alone or served with your favorite soup. I prefer to purchase the ricotta cheese at an Italian market. The ricotta purchased from a grocery store in a plastic tub seems to be too creamy. It does not work well with this recipe.

For the crust, use the recipe in this book.

1 pie crust (top & bottom)
1½ lbs. ricotta cheese 6 large eggs
3 tablespoons grated parmesan cheese
½ teaspoon garlic powder
1 teaspoon dried parsley
½ cup green peas (I prefer frozen, optional)
4 teaspoons bread crumbs
1 teaspoon sea salt
1 teaspoon white pepper

In a mixing bowl, Mix the entire ingredients together gently with a fork, the consistency should resemble lumpy yogurt. It is best to chill for ½ hour before filling the piecrust. I have seen and tasted, other cooks adding fava beans, peas, or chickpeas. It is traditional to do so, but most prefer omitting this ingredient.

Roll out the crust, and spread the crust over a pie pan and fill with the cheese filling.
Top off the pie and with a fork, press the edges sealing the pie.
Poke 5 holes in the top of the crust.
If preferred. For a richer, brown crust, lightly, brush the top with a beaten egg.
Bake in a pre heated 350 degrees oven until the crust turns deep golden brown.

Eggplant Parmigiana

1 medium eggplant, cut into 1/2-inch rounds
½ cup flour
1 egg, lightly beaten
1¼ cups seasoned dry bread crumbs
1 clove garlic, thinly sliced
½ cup olive oil
3 cups Marinara sauce, heated
½ cup fresh basil leaves, thinly sliced
   salt and pepper
¾ cup grated Parmesan cheese
½ pound Mozzarella, thinly sliced

Dip eggplant rounds in the flour, the egg and then in the bread crumbs and transfer to a sheet pan and arrange in a single layer.
In a skillet heat 1/4-inch of olive oil and cook eggplant in batches, adding more olive oil to pan when necessary, until golden brown on both sides.
Transfer cooked eggplant to paper towel-lined sheet pan to drain and season with salt and pepper.
Spread warm marinara sauce in bottom of baking dish and alternate layers of eggplant, marinara sauce, basil, salt and pepper, grated Parmesan cheese and Mozzarella slices, ending with the Mozzarella on top.
Bake in a pre-heated 350 F oven, uncovered, for 30 minutes.

Iris' Caribbean-Style Sofrito

Common in Cuba, Puerto Rico, and the Dominican Republic, sofrito is a blend of herbs and vegetables used in Afro-Latin/Caribbean cooking to season rice, bean, and meat dishes. The ingredient is vegetarian friendly.

2 green bell peppers, cut into 1/4 inch cubes
2 red bell peppers, cut into 1/4 inch cubes
1 orange bell pepper, cut into 1/4 inch cubes
1 yellow bell pepper, cut into 1/4 inch cubes
10 tomatoes, cored and coarsely chopped
1 bunch green onions, chopped
1½ bunches fresh cilantro leaves, chopped
6 fresh tomatillos, husks removed
1 cup chopped garlic

Place the green, red, orange, and yellow bell peppers in a blender or bowl of a food processor. Add the tomatoes, green onions, cilantro, tomatillos, and garlic. Blend or pulse according to your preference to make a chunky or smooth mixture. Refrigerate in a covered container up to 5 days, or freeze up

Mushroom and White Wine Ravioli

I enjoy the flavor of mushroom ravioli in a creamed mushroom sauce. This is an impressive meal to be served with a green salad, and a crisp white wine.

Pastry:
2 cups of flour
1 cup semolina or 1 egg slightly beaten
Dash of salt
Water as necessary to bind dough. Let stand to room temperature

Filling:
1 lb. portabella mushrooms
½ cup finely minced onion
½ cup heavy cream
2 cloves minced garlic
1 tablespoon finely chopped Parsley
1 tablespoon grated cheese
Dash of salt

To make the pastry, mix flour, semolina or egg and salt. Add water
and work into a smooth dough. Rest the dough for one hour.
To make the filling, put all of the ingredients and sauté until creamy, yet stiff.

Divide pastry into four pieces and roll into long strips about for inches wide. Dampen the edges with water. Put about one tablespoon of filling ¾ of and inch from the edge of the pastry and 1-1/2 inches apart. Turn one edge of pastry on the other one and press to seal.

Using a ravioli cutter, cut the pastry ½ inch away from filling.
Set aside on a floured surface about 10 minuets. Boil in salt water in a large pot. In bottom of the pot place saucer upside down. This will prevent the Ravioli from sticking to bottom of pot.

A basic cream sauce infused with morel mushrooms work best for the sauce.

North African Vegetable Stew with Poached Eggs

Who needs any meat after all these vegetables? The eggs are such a nice touch adding another element to the dish. For true vegetarians, omit the eggs.

2 teaspoons extra-virgin olive oil
3 cups frozen pepper stir-fry vegetables
1 teaspoon coriander seeds
½ teaspoon caraway seeds
Pinch of salt
¼ teaspoon paprika
1/8 teaspoon cayenne pepper
4 cloves garlic
1 28-ounce can or 2 14 1/2-ounce cans diced tomatoes
1 19-ounce or 15 1/2-ounce can chickpeas
Freshly ground pepper
4 large eggs

Heat oil in a large nonstick skillet over medium-high heat.
Add stir-fry vegetables; cook, stirring occasionally, until most of the liquid has evaporated, 5 to 7 minutes.
Meanwhile, grind coriander seeds, caraway seeds and salt coarsely in a spice mill, a dry blender or in a mortar and pestle.
Transfer to a small bowl and stir in 1/4 teaspoon paprikas and cayenne.
Add garlic and the spice mixture to the skillet; cook, stirring, for 30 seconds. Add tomatoes and chickpeas; bring to a simmer.
Reduce heat to medium and cook at a lively simmer until slightly thickened, 10 to 15 minutes.
Season with pepper.
Break eggs into separate quadrants of the stew, taking care not to break the yolks. Reduce heat to medium-low, cover the skillet and cook until the eggs are set, 5 to 7 minutes.
Sprinkle eggs with paprika.
Carefully transfer an egg and some stew to each plate.

Vegetarian Moussaka - Ruth Gemus 1973

Moussaka is a layered dish that almost resembles lasagna. This is a vegetarian rendition. The spices used, make this a meal full of flavors that will exploded in your mouth. Don't allow the word vegetarian allude you. Prepare it for anyone.

Preheat oven to 375 degrees

2 large egg plants, sliced 1/2" but not peeled
2 teaspoons salt

Sprinkle both sides of each eggplant slice with salt; place between several thicknesses of paper toweling. Weight down and let stand 1 hour

Tomato Sauce:
3 medium-size onions, peeled and chopped
1 clove garlic, peeled and crushed
2 tablespoons olive or vegetable oil
4 medium size tomatoes, peeled, cored, and coarsely chopped (reserve juice)
¼ teaspoon rosemary leaf, crumbled
2 tablespoons minced fresh mint or 1 tbsp mint flakes
2 teaspoons sugar
1 teaspoon salt
¼ teaspoon pepper
1 can (8oz) tomato sauce

Stir-fry onions and garlic in oil in a large, heavy skillet over moderate heat about 8 minutes, until limp and golden.
Add tomatoes, their juice and all remaining ingredients except tomato sauce and heat, uncovered, stirring occasionally, until tomatoes begin to release their juices. Cover, lower heat and simmer 1 hour, stirring occasionally; stir in tomato sauce and simmer, uncovered, 15 minutes longer.

(Continued)

Cheese Filling:
1 carton (1lb) cream style cottage cheese
1 large egg
2 tablespoons grated parmesan cheese
1/8 teaspoon leaf rosemary crumbled
1/8 teaspoon mace
¼ teaspoon salt
1/8 teaspoon pepper
4 tablespoons olive or vegetable oil
2/3 cup grated parmesan cheese

Mix all ingredients except the 4 tbsp oil and the 2/3 cup parmesan cheese. Refrigerate until needed.

Brush both sides of each eggplant slice lightly with oil, and then broil quickly on each side to brown.

Spoon half the tomato sauce over the bottom of a 13 x 9 x 2 inch baking pan. Sprinkle generously with grated parmesan.

Arrange half the browned egg plant slices on top. Spread with cheese filling, sprinkle with parmesan. Arrange remaining eggplant slices on top.

Sprinkle with parmesan. Finally with the remaining tomato sauce and one last sprinkling of parmesan.

Dish can be prepared to this point several hours ahead of time and refrigerated until about an hour before baking. In fact, it will be better if it is, because the flavors get together better. Bake, uncovered, 45-50 minutes in moderate oven (375 degrees) until bubbling and browned. Remove from oven and let stand 15 minutes before cutting into serving size squares.

Desserts

The end is the last impression your guests will remember

Ambrosia

Everyone has had Ambrosia. Fruits in a creamy tart sauce with nuts. This is a recipe from Lionel Gemus.

Drain Very well:
1 large can fruit cocktail
1 16 oz can pineapple chunks
1 small can mandarin orange slices (optional)

Mix above and then add:
½ cup raisins
1 cup coarsely chopped nuts (preferably walnuts)
2 to 3 cups miniature marshmallows
1 cup shredded coconut
1-1 ½ (16oz) sour cream

If fruits are not drained well, the ambrosia will turn out soupy.

Banana Split Cake

This is a treat for all to enjoy. Everyone loves a banana split, but, now it is a cake! Another recipe perfected by my friend's father Lionel Gemus.

3 sticks margarine butter
2 cups powdered sugar
2 eggs
4 or 5 bananas
1 large can maraschino cherries
1 med. box graham cracker crumbs
9 oz. kool whip (use more if desired)
½ cup chopped nuts

Mix 1 stick melted butter with cracker crumbs in the bottom of a 13 x 2 pan. Pat down evenly and firmly. Over very low heat melt 2 stick butter, 2 well beaten eggs and 2 cups powdered sugar. Cook about 10 minutes and pour over crumb crust. Slice bananas. Spread kool whip over bananas. Sprinkle cherries over kool whip and top with nuts. Cool in refrigerator at least 1 hour before serving (is best over night)

Dennis' Maltese Bread Pudding - Pudina Tal-Hobz

I have tried many recipes for bread pudding. I used a basic recipe and incorporate what ingredients I like most, nuts and fruits. I also like using different types of breads, giving the pudding a marble effect.

1 loaf white bread (Wonder, tastee, silvercup type)
1 loaf cracked wheat bread
1 envelope vanilla pudding mix
½ cup chopped walnuts
½ cup white chocolate chips or peanut butter chips
½ cup sultana raisins
½ cup candied fruit
2 tablespoons vanilla
2 tablespoon almond extract
½ cup milk
2 cans evaporated milk
½ cup sugar

Spread out bread and allow to completely dry out (overnight is best)
Tear the breads and mix in a bowl the pudding sugar almond extract milks and let soak for ½ hour
Mix in all remaining ingredients and bake in a greased pan at 350 degrees for one hour testing the center with a fork or toothpick, should be moist but not wet.
Allow to cool and serve

*Note:
I have made up a simple sauce to serve on top of
1 Cup evaporated milk
2 oz. brandy
Enough powdered sugar to form a sauce

Lionel's Banana's Foster

Banana Forester is probably one of the oldest desert recipes.   Enjoyed by all. The flaming, is a real show piece!

4 large bananas, cut in half length wise, and then halved
4 regular scoops of vanilla ice cream
4 tablespoons butter
1 cup brown sugar
½ teaspoon cinnamon
1 cup brown sugar
4 tablespoon banana liqueur
¼ cup (approx) rum

Melt the butter. As the sugar, cinnamon and banana liqueur and stir to mix. Heat for a few minutes, and then add the bananas and Sautee until soft. Add the rum and allow it to heat well, and then tip the pan so that the flame from a match will cause the sauce to ignite. Allow the sauce to flame until it dies out, tipping the pan with a circular motion to prolong the flame. Serve over vanilla ice cream.
Serves 4

Black Walnut Fancy Cake

The delicate flavor of walnut enhances the cake perfectly. I must admit, it is one of my favorite cake recipes. Serve this desert with a specialty coffee or espresso.

½ cup butter, softened
½ cup shortening
2 cupssugar
5 eggs, separated
1 cup buttermilk
1 teaspoon soda
2 cupsall purpose flour
1 teaspoon vanilla
1½ cups black walnuts
½ teaspoon cream of tarter

Cream butter and shortening. Gradually add sugar, beating until light and fluffy and sugar is dissolved. Add egg yolks and beat well. Combine soda and buttermilk and stir until soda is dissolve. Add flour to creamed mixture, beginning and ending with flour. Add vanilla and walnuts and stir thoroughly.

Beat egg whites (at room temperature) with cream of tartar until stiff peaks form, and then fold into batter. Pour batter into 3 greased and floured 9" cake pans and finish cooling. Frost with cream cheese frosting; and sprinkle top of cake with black walnuts.

CREAM CHEESE FROSTING:
¾ cup butter, softened
8 oz. (1pkge) Cream cheese softened
3 oz. (1pkge) cream cheese softened
6¾ cups sifted powdered sugar
1½ tsp. vanilla

Cream butter and cream cheese, then add sugar gradually and beat until light and fluffy. Add vanilla.

Coffee Liquor Mousse Cake-Lionel Gemus

Just as good as the title. Perfect after an outdoor summer dinner, at your home, to top off the evening. This is a nice touch after serving a grilled meat. I don't suggest serving after a barbequed meats, you may have an overkill of sweetness.

Melted butter for brushing the pan.
Preheat oven to 375 degrees

CAKE:
8 large eggs
1cup sugar
1 cup all purpose flour
1 teaspoon double-acting baking powder
4 tablespoon cocoa powder

Brush a 8-inch round pan, 3 inches in height, with melted butter, line the bottom with a round of wax paper and brush the wax paper also with butter. Next chill the pan for 10 minutes, and when cool, dust both bottom and sides with 4 teaspoons of additional sugar, shaking out the excess.

The next step requires a four quart double boiler. If your double boiler has only two quart capacity, split the cake ingredients to half the quantity and make it twice to come up to the desired quantity.

In the top of the 4 quart double boiler set over barely simmering water, beat 8 eggs and 1 cup of sugar with an electric mixer for 10 minutes or until the mixture is light and foamy. Transfer the mixture to a bowl, sift the baking powder and 4 tablespoons of cocoa powder over the top and fold in (do not stir) the dry ingredients. Pour the batter into the pan and bake the cake in a preheated 375 degrees oven for approximately 25 minutes or until the cake tester comes out dry.

Let the cake cool for 4 minutes, turn it out on a rack and let it cool completely.

(Continued)

MOUSSE:
5 tablespoons cocoa powder
¼ cup coffee liqueur or kahlua
4 cups whipping cream, well chilled
1 cup sugar

In a chilled large bowl beat cream until it is foamy, beat in the 1 cup of sugar, a little at a time, and beat until the cream holds soft peaks. Sift in the 5tbsp of cocoa powder, the ¼ cup coffee liqueur and beat mixture until it hold stiff peaks. Transfer 2/3 cups of the mousse to a pastry bag fitted with a decorative tip.

Split the cake horizontally into 5 layers. Transfer one layer to a cake plate. With a pastry brush, spread with ¼ inch of mousse. Next place second layer over first layer, and repeat with the liqueur and mousse. Repeat this process with the next three layers. You should have enough mousse to cover the very top and sides.

Pipe stars or other decorative designs around the rim of the top layer.

This cake seems best if done a day ahead and refrigerated. It can also be frozen for later use.

Maltese Almond Macaroons   (Biskuttini Tal-Lewz)

I don't think this is so much Maltese cookie. It is the basic recipe for the traditional macaroon cookie. But don't let that discourage you, they are delicious.

2 egg whites
2/3 cups refined sugar
1-1/3 cups shredded coconut
2 tablespoons ground almonds
½ teaspoon almond extract
¼ teaspoon vanilla
dash of salt

Beat egg white, salt, vanilla, almond extract until soft peaks form. Add sugar gradually, continue beating until still.
Fold in almonds and coconut
Drop onto a greased cookie sheet, from a teaspoon.
Bake at 325 degrees for 20 – 25 minutes

Date Slices   (Imqaret)

My Grandmother would prepare these sweet morsels every New Year's eve. When the clock struck midnight we as a family would welcome in the New Year with a shot of Anisette Liquor and the date slices, no matter what age we were.

Pastry:
2 cups all purpose flour
½ cup butter
¼ teaspoon baking powder
3 tablespoons sugar
1 egg
1 tablespoon Anisette liquor
3 tablespoons COLD water

Filling:
1 lb. dates cut into small squares
¼ teaspoon orange extract
¼ teaspoon lemon extract
¼ cup Anisette liquor
¼ cup chopped nuts (optional)
1 cup grated orange rind
1 cup grated lemon rind
3 tablespoons Water

Pastry:
Mix butter, flour and baking powder together with a fork, until completely mixed. Add egg, anisette and sugar. Add water. Mix on medium in a mixes with a dough hook until a smooth ball is formed. Set aside covered in a clean damp towel for 1 hour at room temp.

Filling:
Place all other ingredients in a deep saucepan with three tablespoons of water and heat to a simmer, stir to a lumpy paste.

Roll out dough into long strips about four inches wide and brush the edges with water. Place filling in the center and flip the dough over the filling sealing by pressing the wet edges together. With a sharp knife every 1 ½ inches and fry in a frying pan 1/3 filled with a good grade of vegetable oil, until golden brown.

Remove and place on several paper towel to drain. Dust the top with powder sugar. Best served when warm.

You may bake instead of fry in a 350 degree oven for 20 – 25 minutes.

Mississippi Mud
Only one way to describe this rich layered creation of dessert. Heaven.

FOUR LAYERS:

2 small cool whips
1-8 oz. Philadelphia cream cheese
2 packages (small) Jell-O instant choc pudding
½ cup or more chopped nuts
  Choc bits for decoration
1 cup flour
1 stick margarine
1 cup powdered sugar
2½ cups whole milk

First Layer:
1 cup flour
Pinch salt
1 stick margarine
½ cup nuts (or more) chopped

Mix well, mash into bottom of 13" oblong pan, bake at 350 degrees
Until lightly tan.

Second Layer:
1 8oz. Philadelphia cream cheese
1 cup powdered sugar
1 mix well, spread over 1st layer with wet flat knife or spatula

Third Layer:
2 packages (small) instant choc pudding
2 ½ cups homogenized milk
 Mix with wire whip and spread over layer #2

Fourth Layer:
Top with small cool whip. Garnish with choc bits and more pecans if desired. Put in ice box to set. (2 or more hours).

One thousand calories per bite and worth every one of them.

PECAN ROLLS - (SHORTBREAD COOKIES)

Nice for the children. This recipe is fast and easy.

1 lb. butter
8 tablespoons XXX sugar
2 tablespoons pure Vanilla
2 cups crushed pecans

Cream 1 lb. butter with 8 tbsp. xxx sugar.
Add 2 teaspoons vanilla, 4 cups all purpose flour and 2 cups of crushed pecans. Roll in hands into very tiny balls or sausage or crescent shapes. Place on ungreased cookie sheet and bake at 225 degrees for 45 minutes. Roll in xxx sugar while hot. These should not brown.

Pumpkin Bread

Pumpkin bread is desert bread with the traditional spices. I always serve this type of bread with a few flavored butters and cream cheese spreads. Try them all, from fruits to herbs to different cheese flavors. Works well in the morning.

3 cups sugar
3 ½ cups flour
2 teaspoons soda
½ teaspoon salt
2 teaspoons each:
   Allspice, nutmeg, cloves, and cinnamon
4 large eggs
2 cups pumpkin
1 cup oil
1 cup water (or ½ cup water plus ½ cup rum, brandy or cherry liquor)
1 cup raisins
1 cup pecans

Combine sugar, flour, soda, salt, allspice, nutmeg, cloves, and cinnamon.
Mix eggs, pumpkin, oil, water, rum, and combine with dry ingredients, mixing well.
Fold in pecans and raisins.
Bake in greased bundt pan 1hr-15mins at 325 degrees-or bake in greased 1lb.

coffee cans 45 minutes at 325 degrees.
Let cool in pan for approximately 15 minutes before removing. Sift confectioners sugar on top while warm.

Robin's Christmas Cake

My favorite holiday cake. Best served warm (microwave slightly) with a hot beverage. If you decide to soak the cake in a liquor, plan on making the recipe weeks before. I have soaked a cake in a whiskey soaked towel, placed in a cake tin and allowed it to soak until the next year's Christmas table. It was great! Just make sure if you do this, the tin is air tight and in a cool dry place.

12 oz. box pitted dates, cut in half crosswise
½ lb. mixed candied green and yellow pine apple cut in coarse pieces
1lb. whole candied cherries
1 cup cake flour
1 teaspoon baking powder
¼ teaspoon salt
2 large eggs
½ cup white sugar
1lb. pecan halves
1 cup liquor (optional)

Grease 9" tube pan well. Line bottom with wax paper and grease again over the wax paper. Set aside.
Combine dates, pineapple and cherries in large mixing bowl. Stir together flour, baking powder and salt. Sprinkle over fruit and mix well with fingers, spreading pieces of fruit to coat well. Beat eggs and sugar until light and fluffy. Pour over fruit and mix well with spoon. Add pecans and mix with hands until pecans are evenly distributed and coated well with batter.
Pack in pan, pressing down with hands moistened with cold water. If necessary, rearrange fruit and nuts to distribute evenly. Bake at 275 degrees for about one and a quarter (1-1/4) hours. Top of cake should look dry but not brown. Cool pan on rack 5 minutes. Loosen edges around tube with spatula. Then invert on rack peel off paper and turn cake top-side up. Cool thoroughly.
I like to wrap the cake in a liquor soaked towel for at least one week. If you choose to do so, I found it best to store in cake tins. I use a cheap whiskey, but I have also used different fruit liquors. Do no use any clear liquor or sour fruit (sour apple snapps et.) they do not go well with the cake at all.
Wrap air tight and store in cool place. Cake improves with storing. Decorate on top if you wish with candied fruit. To cut, you need a very sharp knife or preferably an electric knife.

Robin's Easy and Quick Trifle

Quick and easy, the most time spent is waiting for the gelatin to stiffen. Robin sometimes uses sugarless products so that Diabetics can have some too.

2 packages any flavor Jell-O
2 packages any flavor pudding
1 lb. angel food cake
2 tubs non dairy whip topping

This is simple and easy to follow:
On the bottom of a baking dish prepare the gelatin as described on the package. Wait to stiffen, in a separate bowl prepare the pudding, and pour over the stiff gelatin.
Top with crumbles of angel food cake
Top with the whip topping
Garnish with colored sugar sprinkles or some type of slivered nuts.

Sesame Rings   (Qaghaq Tal-Gulglien)

This is a traditional Maltese cookie. The orange rinds bring out an aroma and flavor like no other. A cookie that is not too sweet but simply perfect for dipping into a cup of hot tea as most Maltese do. Or a late night snack, anytime is a good time for Qaghaq Tal-Gulglien!
(Ah-Tal-Jun-Jlen)

4 cups flour
¾ cup sugar
2 teaspoons baking powder
2 eggs
½ cup orange rind
½ lb. butter (soft)
¼ cup milk
2 teaspoons anise seeds
½ cup sesame seeds (reserve)

In a bowl, put ingredients as listed except for sesame seed. Mix well. Take small Pieces of dough and roll into long strips about 4 inches long and ½ inch wide. Now bring two ends of pastry together to form a ring or loop.

Put the sesame seeds in small bowl or dish. Dip the rings or loops in the sesame seeds.

Put them on an un-greased cookie sheet. Bake at 400 degrees for about 15 minutes.

(I prefer leaving them just a little time longer, so that they are browned on the bottom.

Makes about four dozen.

For information:
HeavyD95@Wowway.com